Abir KHALDI

DevOps for beginners

Abir KHALDI

DevOps for beginners

Practical courses and workshops

ScienciaScripts

Imprint

Any brand names and product names mentioned in this book are subject to trademark, brand or patent protection and are trademarks or registered trademarks of their respective holders. The use of brand names, product names, common names, trade names, product descriptions etc. even without a particular marking in this work is in no way to be construed to mean that such names may be regarded as unrestricted in respect of trademark and brand protection legislation and could thus be used by anyone.

Cover image: www.ingimage.com

This book is a translation from the original published under ISBN 978-3-8416-3786-4.

Publisher:
Sciencia Scripts
is a trademark of
Dodo Books Indian Ocean Ltd. and OmniScriptum S.R.L publishing group

120 High Road, East Finchley, London, N2 9ED, United Kingdom
Str. Armeneasca 28/1, office 1, Chisinau MD-2012, Republic of Moldova, Europe
Printed at: see last page
ISBN: 978-620-8-21254-4

Contents

Introduction

DevOps, short for 'development' and 'operations', has become a ubiquitous term, often cited but sometimes misunderstood. While many talk about it, few really understand its depth. In reality, DevOps is based on Lean and Agile principles, with the emphasis on collaboration between business, development, operations and quality assurance teams. The central objective is to enable continuous software delivery, so as to respond more quickly to market opportunities and better integrate user feedback.

Enterprise information systems are becoming increasingly complex, integrating a wide range of technologies, databases and user environments. This growing complexity can only be effectively managed through a DevOps approach. However, the definition and interpretation of DevOps varies from one point of view to another. Some see it as a methodology reserved for technical experts, while others associate this approach primarily with the adoption of the Cloud.

Still others consider that DevOps goes far beyond technical services and has established itself as a true business approach. It's a software delivery method that takes charge of each function, from its initial design to its release, while delivering tangible value to end-users. To be successful, this approach requires the active participation of all stakeholders: not only development and operations teams, but also users, business line managers, partners and suppliers. A true DevOps culture embraces the entire organisation, transcending the traditional boundaries of technical departments.

About this book

This book has been designed to give you an in-depth view of DevOps, covering its key concepts as well as the technologies that support it. It combines clear explanations with practical workshops to reinforce both your theoretical and technical skills. You will discover the essential steps and tools for implementing an effective DevOps approach, tailored to the needs of today's market. Thanks to the practical exercises, you'll have the opportunity to put your knowledge into practice and master the methods that are essential in this constantly changing world.

Who this book is for

This book is aimed at beginners, professionals looking to improve their skills and students of information technology. Whether you're just starting out in your career, changing careers, or already have some experience, this book will guide you step by step, with concrete examples and practical workshops, to help you master the principles and tools of DevOps. It is designed for those who want to evolve in a constantly changing environment and improve their ability to respond quickly to market needs.

Organisation of the work

This book is structured to provide you with a progressive and complete understanding of DevOps, alternating between theory and practice.

Chapitre 1   ***Principles of the DevOps movement***

This first chapter introduces the fundamental principles of DevOps, exploring its origins, objectives and impact on development and operational practices. You will discover how this method facilitates effective collaboration between teams for continuous software delivery.

Chapitre 2   ***Source management***

The second chapter focuses on version and source management, a crucial aspect in ensuring the coherence and traceability of developments. It discusses best practice and associated tools, while providing practical exercises for applying these concepts.

Chapitre 3   ***: Build tools***

In this chapter, we'll look at the build tools that are essential for automating the compilation and deployment of applications. You will learn how to configure and use these tools to optimise your build processes, with practical workshops to reinforce your understanding.

Chapitre 4   ***Containers with Docker***

The fourth chapter is dedicated to containers, with a focus on Docker. You will discover how Docker simplifies the management of deployment environments and how to integrate it into your DevOps workflows. Practical examples will help you master the use of containers.

Chapitre 5   ***: Jenkins***

Finally, the fifth chapter looks at Jenkins, a clb tool for continuous integration and continuous deployment. You will learn how to configure and use Jenkins to automate your deployment pipelines, with practical exercises to put your new skills into practice.

Each chapter combines theoretical explanations with practical workshops, enabling you to develop concrete skills while consolidating your theoretical knowledge. This alternation between theory and practice is designed to prepare you effectively to apply DevOps concepts in real environments.

## Chapter 1

Principles of the DevOps movement

Introduction

In 2024, DevOps continues to redefine the technology landscape, with impressive figures attesting to its impact and growing adoption. According to Puppet's "State of DevOps Report 2024", organisations that adopt DevOps experience a significant improvement in their performance. In particular, these companies show a 46 times higher dëploiement frequency and a 2.6 times higher dëploiement success rate than non-adopting companies. In addition, these organisations reduce their delivery cycle times by 50%, enabling them to react more quickly to market needs.

The "Global DevOps Market Report 2024" from MarketsandMarkets indicates that the DevOps market is valued at around $20 billion in 2024, with forecast growth of 22% per year until 2028. This rapid growth is largely due to increased demand for solutions that enable continuous software delivery and improved collaboration between development and operations teams.

In terms of tools, Docker is now used by 70% of Fortune 500 companies to manage containers, making applications more portable and scalable. **Jenkins**, one of the most widely used continuous integration tools, is deployed by 55% of large companies to automate their deployment pipelines, helping to reduce errors and accelerate development cycles.

Current figures clearly demonstrate that DevOps practices are no longer an option, but a necessity for companies seeking to maintain a competitive edge in a constantly evolving technology market. The growing adoption of these practices and tools bears witness to their value in optimising software development and deployment processes.

The DevOps method

The term DevOps was first used by Patrick Debois and Andrew Shafer during their "Agile Infrastructure" conference at the 2008 Agile Toronto Conference.

DevOps is a movement and an approach that favours close collaboration between development (Dev) and operations (Ops) teams for all information technology solutions. The aim is to improve the quality of the work and the relationship between these two teams, each with its own vision for achieving customer satisfaction. These practices enable applications to be developed, tested and delivered more quickly and with greater reliability.

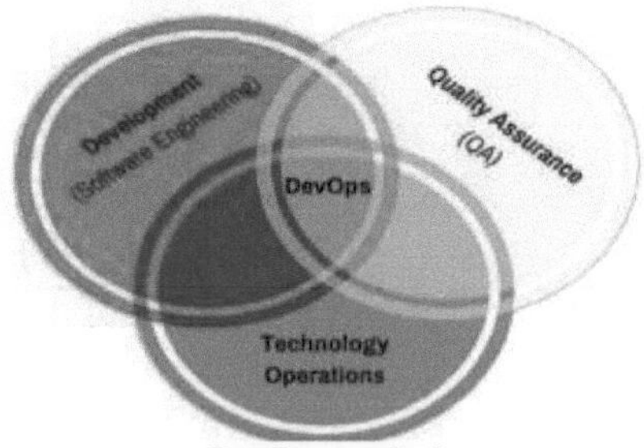

- DevOps method -

Relationship between Dev and Ops

Collaboration between development (Dev) and operations (Ops) teams is essential for success in a DevOps environment.

The Dev teams, made up of software developers, focus on creating and improving applications. They are responsible for writing code, developing new features and resolving bugs.

At the same time, the Ops teams, responsible for putting products into production, ensure the deployment, management and maintenance of applications in production. Their role includes managing infrastructures, monitoring systems and guaranteeing the availability and performance of applications.

By adopting a DevOps approach, these two teams work together in a more integrated way, sharing common goals and responsibilities throughout the application lifecycle. This synergy not only speeds up the dëveloppement and deployment cycles, but also improves product stability and quality, while responding more effectively to end-users' needs.

- Dev and Ops relationship -

The antagonism between development (Dev) and operations (Ops) teams is often marked by sometimes divergent objectives.

Dev teams aim to make changes at the lowest possible cost and in the shortest possible time, seeking to introduce new functionality quickly and solve problems in an agile way.

Ops teams, on the other hand, focus on the stability of the system and the quality of operations, ensuring that the applications deployed are reliable, high-performing and continuously available. This tension between rapid deployment and the need to maintain high quality and stability can create friction. However, the DevOps approach seeks to mitigate these conflicts by encouraging closer collaboration between the two teams, aligning their objectives to balance speed of innovation and operational stability.

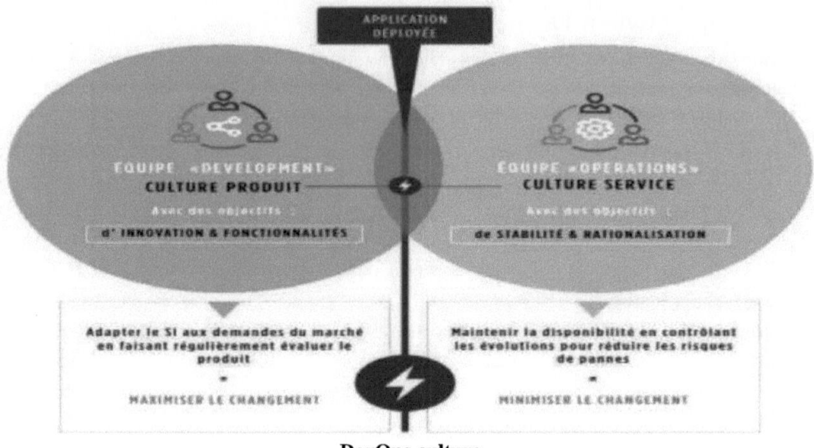

- DevOps culture -

Agile vs DevOps

■ Agile methods are based on pragmatism and iterative development. They define a less rigid framework than traditional methods.

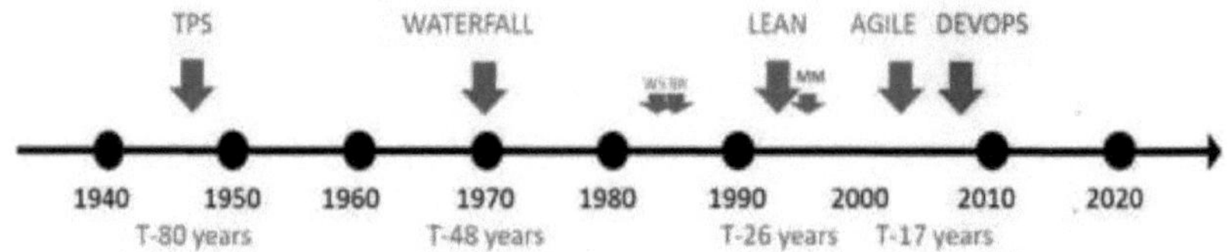

■ The agile method also recommends shorter software development cycles, as opposed to traditional "cascade" methods.

■ The agile methodology reduces risk, repeating shorter design, coding and test cycles that can resolve any surprises and correct the project in progress as early as possible.

■ Numerous **DevOps** approaches, in particular **Scrum** and **Kanban**, incorporating elements of agile programming.

■ In the agile method, **deployment to production** always takes place **at the end of** the project. This explains the lack of collaboration between the two teams, developers and operations.

■ In the DevOps method, the Dev team's work doesn't end when a new version (or bug fix) of the application is released. They must also work with the Ops team to test, deploy and measure its Key Performance Indicator (KPI).

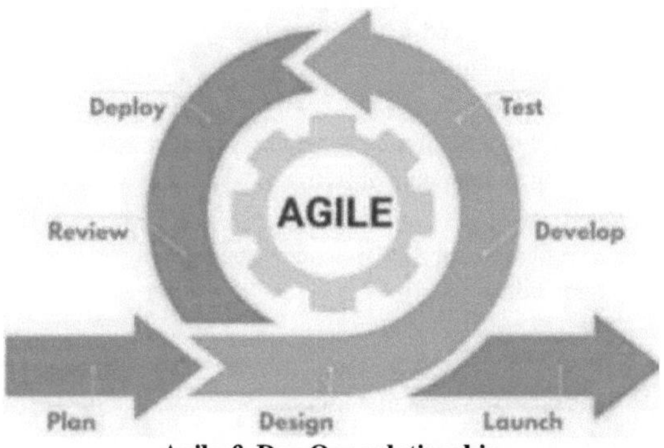

- Agile & Dev Ops relationship -

DevOps - How it works

■   The *DevOps* approach aims to reconcile the two teams, Dev and Ops, by creating a culture of **collaboration** based on shared objectives and projects, and on delivering value.

■   DevOps principles (**CALMS**) :

Culture: Understanding and improving the values and attitudes of the business environment in the service of development.

Automation:Everything that can be **automated** should be.

Lean: Saving **costs** and eliminating unnecessary resources.

Measure: Quickly locate software errors and analyse user behaviour by implementing information feedback systems.

Sharing : Sharing and communication between teams.

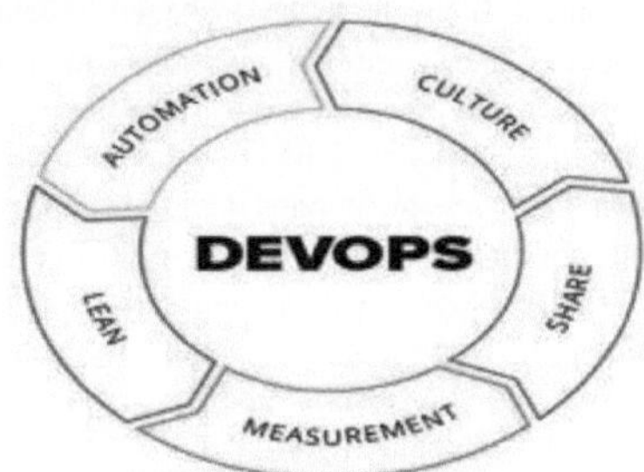

- DevOps principle -

Benefits of DevOps

■   *Acceleration of development cycles*

o DevOps reduces the time to market for products through increased automation and better collaboration between development and operations teams.

■   *Improving software quality*

o DevOps practices encourage continuous testing and integration, which leads to early detection of errors and improved code quality.

■   *Deployments more frequently*

o With tools like continuous integration and continuous deployment, DevOps facilitates more frequent and reliable deployments, enabling regular updates and continuous improvements.

■   *Cost reduction*

o Automating the development, test and deployment processes reduces the costs associated with human error and delays, while optimising resources.

- ***Better collaboration and communication***
o DevOps fosters a culture of collaboration between development and operations teams, improving communication, reducing friction and aligning objectives.

- ***Reducing recovery time***
o In the event of a fault or problem, DevOps practices enable rapid response and effective incident resolution, reducing application downtime.

- ***Scalability and flexibility***
o The use of containers and orchestration tools enables better management of environments, facilitating scalability and adaptation to changing user needs.

- ***Better visibility and control***
o DevOps tools provide greater visibility of the development and deployment process, enabling real-time monitoring of performance and incidents.

- ***Increased Customer Satisfaction***
o By accelerating the application lifecycle and responding rapidly to user feedback, DevOps contributes to greater customer satisfaction and rapid adaptation to market requirements.

- ***Continuous Innovation***
o Implementing DevOps encourages a culture of innovation by enabling teams to rapidly test and deploy new ideas and functionalities.

These benefits show how DevOps can transform software development processes and improve the overall efficiency of IT operations.

CI/CD pipeline

A CI/CD (Continuous Integration/Continuous Deployment) pipeline is a set of automated processes that enable the software development lifecycle to be managed efficiently, from code writing to production deployment. Continuous Integration (CI) involves automating the merging of code developed by different team members into a central repository several times a day. Each integration triggers automated tests to check the quality and functionality of the code, enabling errors to be detected quickly and a stable code base to be maintained. Continuous Deployment (CD) takes over by automating the delivery of valid code to production or pre-production environments. This enables frequent and reliable updates to be deployed with a minimum of manual intervention. Together, CI/CD reduces the time between developing new functionality and putting it into production, improves software quality through continuous testing, and ensures a rapid response to market needs, while minimising the risks associated with deployment.

Continuous Integration (CI)

- *THIS* is a practice that allows code to be integrated with other developers
- Most often, the integration of the code is to check that the build stage is still functional.
- A common practice is also to check that the unit tests (Unit Testing stage) are still functional.
- The aim of the *CI* pipeline is to build a **package** that can then be deployed.

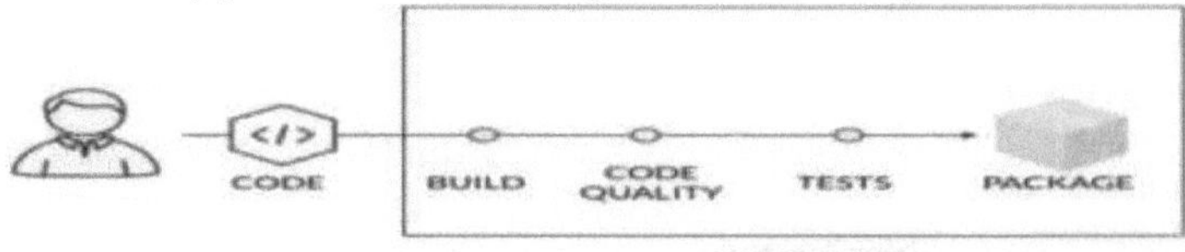

Continuous Delivery (CD)

- It's an extension of continuous integration

■ The purpose of the CD is to take the package created by the CI pipeline and test its deployment in a **test environment (REVIEW and STAGING).**

■ By adding this pre-production stage and running certain tests, we can run different types of test that require the entire system to respond (generally known as acceptance tests).

■ The production deployment stage (STAGE DEPLOY) is launched **manually** if, and only if, the package has successfully passed through all the previous stages.

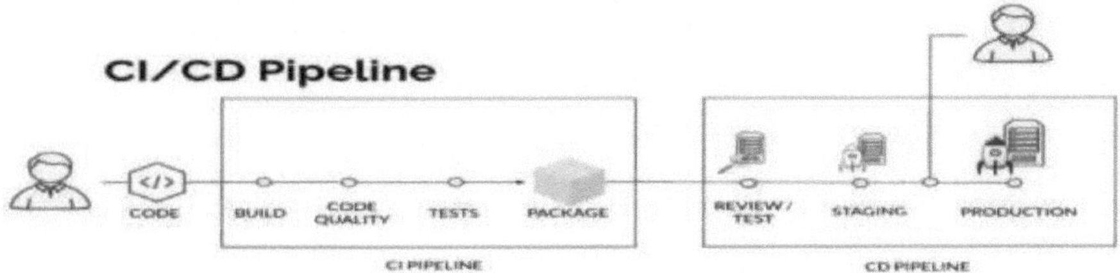

Continuous Deployment (CD)

■ Continuous deployment is the practice of fully automating all CI/CD pipeline processes in a **production** environment.

■ The package must first pass through all the previous stages successfully

■ No manual intervention is required: **the system automatically**

Continuous Integration and Continuous Delivery (CI/CD)

■ Continuous integration will take place in 5 stages:

1. **Plan** your development.
2. **Compile** and integrate your code.
3. **Test** your code.
4. Measure the **quality** of your code.
5. Manage your application's **deliverables**.

■ To set up **continuous delivery**, you need to implement **5 steps**:

1. Infrastructure coding with **Infrastructure-as-Code**.
2. Deploying your application.
3. **Testing** your application in a test environment.
4. Application **supervision**.
5. Setting up alert **notifications**.

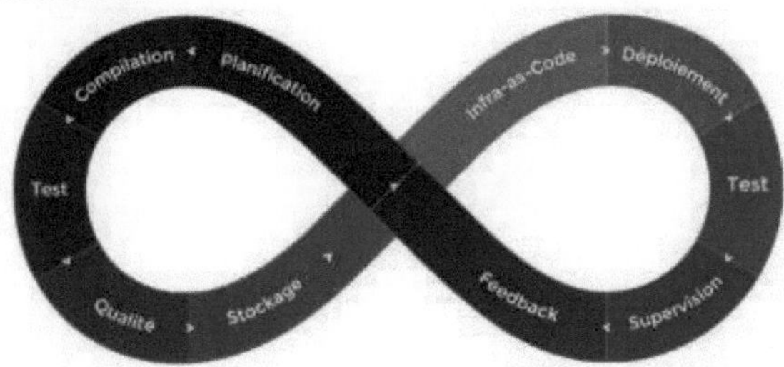

- **DevOps Cycle -**

Infrastructure as Code

■ Infrastructure as Code, laC is a type of IT infrastructure that operations teams can **automatically manage** and **provision** via code, rather than using a manual or interactive process.

■ Infrastructure as code is sometimes referred to as **programmable** infrastructure.

■ LaC offers many advantages over manual provisioning: it can be controlled, version tested and leads to faster software provisioning and delivery.

CI Tools

■ **Planning:** To collaborate with your teams, you can use **Jira**, **GitLab**, **Confluence**, ALM Octane or Pivotal Tracker.

■ **Source code control: Git**, **Subversion**, **GitHub**, **GitLab**, Perforce and **Bitbucket** are the tools for source control.

■ **The orchestrator:** You can orchestrate the stages of your continuous integration using tools such as **Jenkins**, TeamCity, Azure DevOps, **GitLab CI**, Concours CI, Travis CI or **Bamboo**.

■ **Compiling:** You can compile your code with **Maven**, **Ant**, **Gradle**, MSBuild, NAnt, Gulp or Grunt.

■ **Testing the code:** To implement and run your unit tests, you'll find tools like **JUnit**, NUnit and XUnit.

■ **Measuring code quality:** Code quality can be assessed using **SonarQube**, Cast or GitLab Code Quality.

■ **Manage the application's deliverables:** Artifacts can be made available via **Nexus**, **Artifactory**, **GitLab repository**, Quay, Docker Hub.

CD Tools

■ **Codifying infrastructure with Infrastructure-as-Code:** The main Infrastructure-as-Code tools are **Docker**, **Chef**, **Puppet**, **Ansible** and **Terraform**.

■ **Deploy the application:** To deploy the artefacts you created earlier, you can use **Spinnaker**, **XLDeploy** or **UrbanCode**.

■ **Test your application:**

■ **Acceptance test**: you can use **Confluence**, **FitNesse** or **Ranorex**.

■ **Performance testing:** you can use **JMeter**, **Apache Bench** or **Gatling**.

■ **Smoke test:** you can use **Selenium**, **SoapUI** or **Cypress** to check that the application is working properly.

■ **Monitoring application behaviour:** to monitor your applications, you can use the **Elastic**, **Prometheus** or **Graylog** suite.

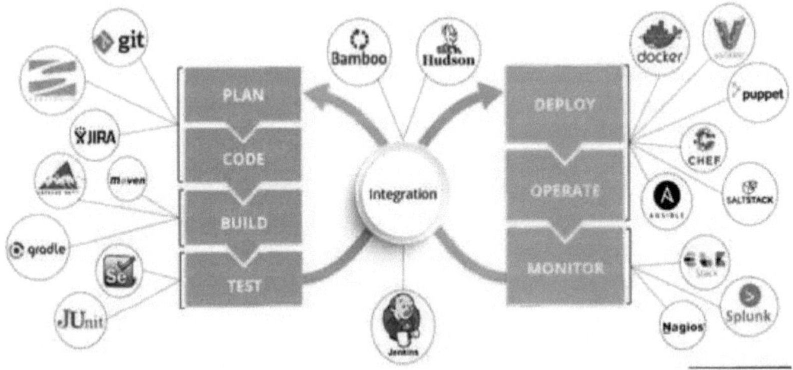

- DevOps tools -

## Chapter 2

Source management

Version control

- Version Control (*VC*), also known as Revision Control (RC), is the practice of tracking and managing changes or modifications to source code.
- A developer can propose several revisions a day
- For every IT project, you need a **backup strategy**

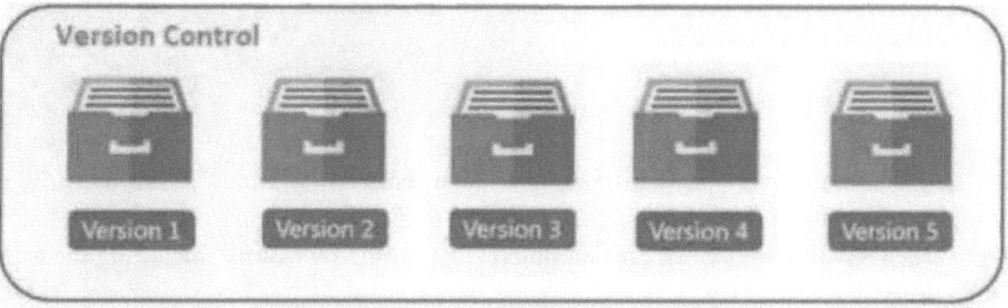

Source code control management systems (SCMS)

- Source code control management systems (SCMS) provide a **continuous history** of code development and help **resolve conflicts** when merging contributions from multiple sources.

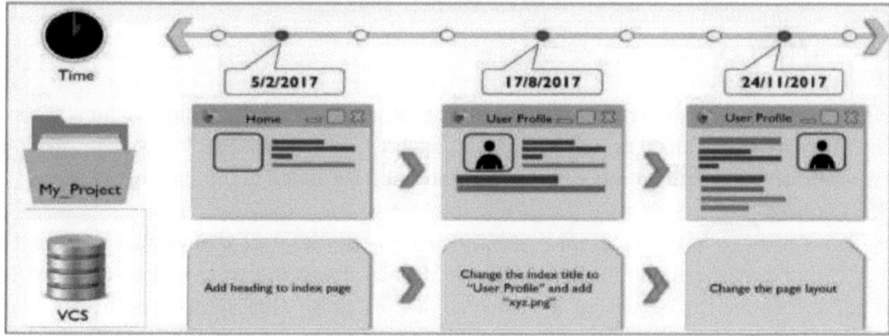

- *SCM* software is sometimes called :
- Version Control System (VCS)
- Source Code Manager System (SCMS)
- Revision Control System (RCS)

Types of source code control management systems (SCMS)

There are two versioning models:

- *Centralized model*: the software code is managed by a central server.

Examples: SVN, CVS

- *Distributed model*: all developers have access to the code without going through a server.

Examples: Git, Mercurial, Bazaar

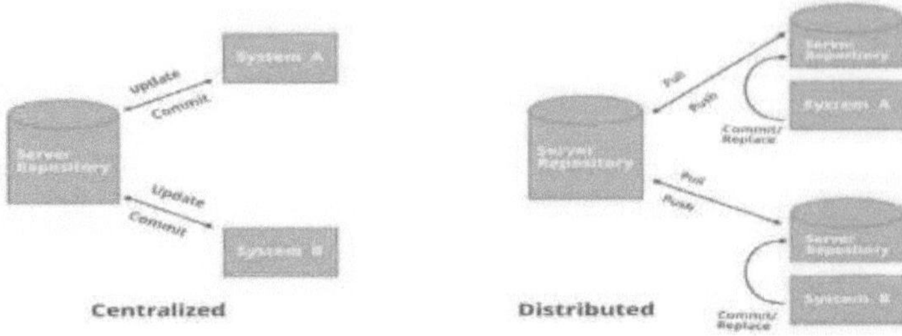

GIT

Presentation

Git is a distributed version management system, created by Linus Torvalds in 2005, used primarily for software development. Unlike centralised version management systems, Git allows each developer to work on a complete copy of the repository, including the full history of the project.

This decentralised approach facilitates collaboration between teams, improves flexibility and ensures data security by enabling offline operations and offering powerful mechanisms for managing branches and mergers.

Git has become an essential tool for versioning code, with widespread adoption in the software development industry.

Key concepts of Git

1. Working Directory

The working directory is where the project files are stored on your local machine. This is where you make your changes and where the files are visible and editable. Changes made in the working directory are not yet saved in Git until they are added to the staging area.

2. Staging Area

The staging area, or index, is an intermëdiary area where you place the changes you want to include in the next commit. When you use the 'git add' command, you prepare the modified files for the commit, plagiarising them in the staging area. This allows you to group the changes together and save them in a single cohërente opëration.

3. Local Repository (Dëp6t Local)

The local dëp6t is where Git stores versions of your project. It contains the complete commit history, including branches and tags. When you make a commit, Git saves the changes from the staging area in the local dëp6t. This allows you to revert to earlier versions of the project if necessary.

4. Remote Repository

The remote repository is a version of the local repository stored on an external server, often hosted on platforms such as GitHub, GitLab or Bitbucket. It enables several developers to work together by synchronising changes using the 'git push' and 'git pull' commands.

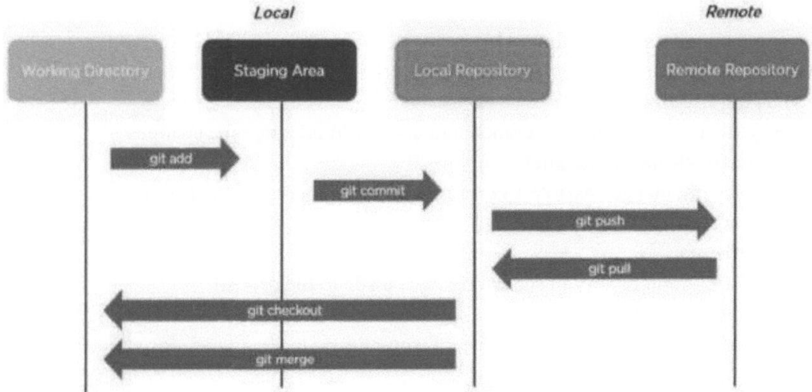

Git steps

1. **Depot initialisation**

- Create a new Git repository or convert an existing directory into a Git repository.
- Command: **git init**
- Example: **git init** creates a new Git repository in the current directory.

2. **Cloning the Depot**

- Clone a remote dëp6t to obtain a complete local copy of the project.
- Command: **git clone [URL]**
- Example: **git clone** https://github.com/username/repository.git copies the remote d6pot to your local machine.

3. **Change Management**

- Add files to the staging area, make commits to save changes in the local d6pot, and manage the branches.
- Command: **git add [file]**
- Example: **git add index.html** adds the file 'index.html' to the staging area for the next commit.
- Command: **git commit -m "[message]"'**
- Example: '**git commit -m "Add new feature"** saves changes to the staging area with the commit message "Add new feature".

4. **Synchronisation with the Remote Depot**

- R6cup6rez and send the changes between your local d6pot and the remote d6pot.
- Command: **git pull**
- Example: **git pull origin main** retrieves changes from the 'main' branch of the remote d6pot and merges them with the local branch.
- Command: **git push**
- Example: **git push origin main** sends local commits from the 'main' branch to the remote d6pot.

5. Branch Management

- Create, delete and manage branches to organise feature development.
- Command: **git branch**
- Example: **git branch** lists all local branches. **git branch feature-xyz'** creates a new

branch called 'feature-xyz'.
- Command: **git checkout [branch]**
- Example: **'git checkout feature-xyz'** changes the current branch to 'feature-xyz'.
6. Merging Modifications
- Merge the changes from one branch into another to integrate the changes.
- Command: **git merge [branch]**
- Example: **git merge feature-xyz** merges changes made to the 'feature-xyz' branch into the current branch.
7. View History
- View the commit history to see the changes made to the deposit.
- Command: **git log**
- Example : **git log** displays the list of commits with detailed information about each commit.

Git Flow

Git Flow is a branch management method that structures development in several distinct stages to improve organisation and version management. Here are the main branches used in Git Flow :

- **Master**: Main branch containing the code ready for production. Stable versions of the project are published from this branch.
- **Develop**: Branch of development that integrates new features and bug fixes before they are released. This is the basis for future versions of the product.
- **Feature**: Temporary branches created to develop new functionality. They are derived from 'develop' and merged into 'develop' once completed.
- **Release**: Branches used to prepare a new stable version. They are used to make the final adjustments before merging into the 'master'.
- **Hotfix**: Branches created to quickly correct critical problems in 'master'. They are used to resolve urgent bugs and are merged into both 'master' and 'develop'.

Git with a remote repository

A remote repository is a version of a project hosted on a server, enabling several users to collaborate and synchronise their work. Remote repositories are generally hosted on platforms such as GitHub, GitLab or Bitbucket. Working with a remote repository involves retrieving (pull) the latest modifications, sending (push) new contributions, and managing collaboration between several developers.

Here is an example of a remote depot workflow:

1. **Clone a remote repository**: git clone https://github.com/user/repo.git to copy a remote dëpôt locally.

2. **Synchronising the repository**: Before starting work, we recommend running git pull origin main to retrieve the latest changes from the main branch.

3. **Pushing changes** : After addingb (git add) and committing (git commit) the changes, you can send them to the remote dbpot with git push origin main.

In short, using a remote dbpot facilitates collaboration between teams and ensures that everyone is working on the most up-to-date version of the project, while ensuring that changes are traceable.

The figure above gives a clear overview of how Git works.

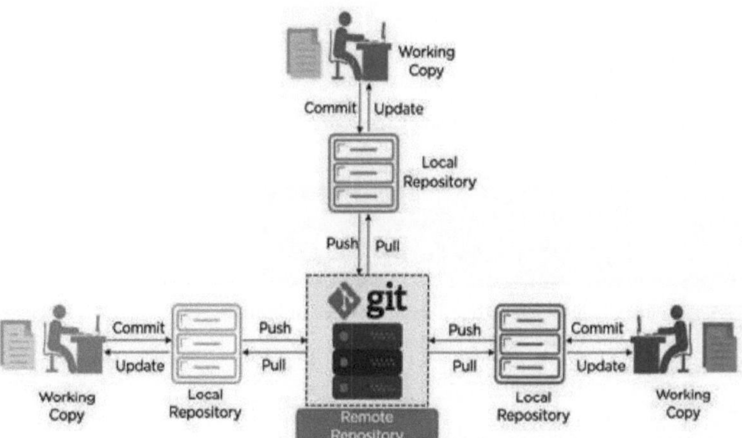

- How Git works -

<h1 align="center">Workshop 1. Using Git</h1>

Step 1: Installing Git

1.   Open the Ubuntu terminal.
2.   Check if Git is already installed by running the command

```
git --version
```

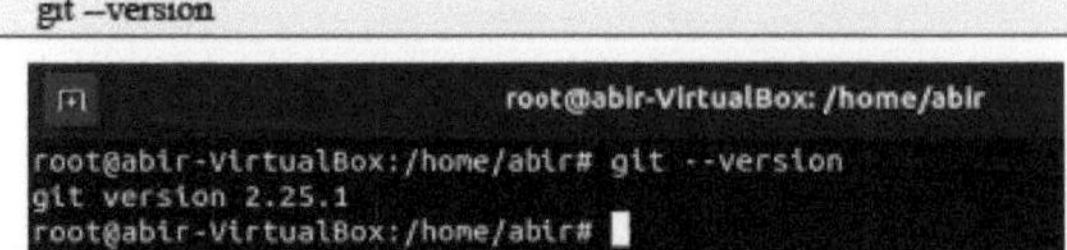

In our case, git is already installed on our ubuntu machine in version 2.25.1.

If Git is not installed, install it using the command :

```
sudo apt update

sudo apt install git
```

Check the Git version again to confirm the installation:

```
git --version
```

Step 2: Initial Git configuration

1.   Configure your Git username

```
git config --global user.name "Votre Nom"
```

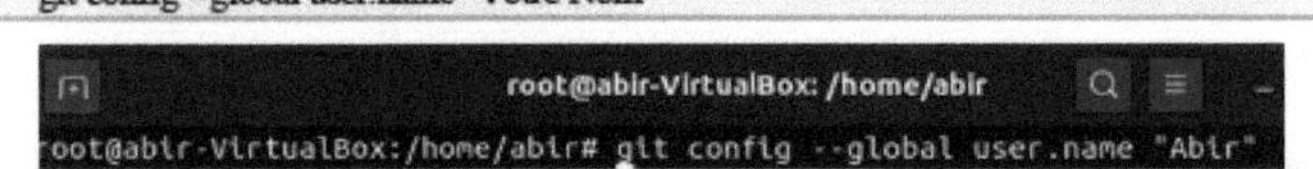

2.   Configure your Git email address :

```
git config --global user.email "votre@email.com"
```

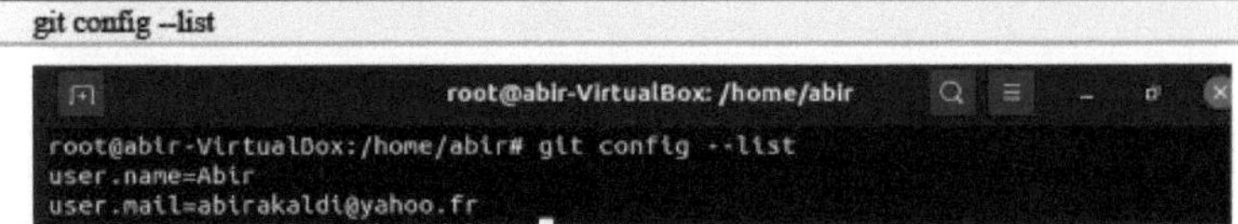

3.   Check the Git configuration :

```
git config --list
```

Step 3: Creating a new Git repository

1.   Create a new folder for your project called **RepProjectTest**:

```
mkdir RepProjectTest

cd RepProjectTest
```

2.   Initialize a new Git repository in this folder :

```
git init
```

The **RepProjectTest** project is initialized with git .

We can browse the files in the .git directory with the command.

```
ls .git
```

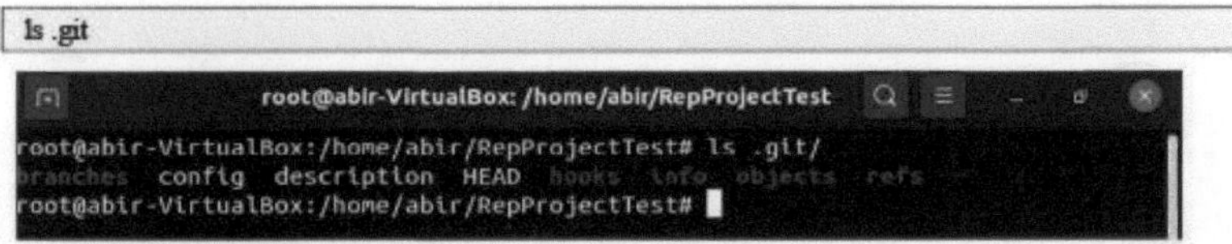

Descriptions of the contents of .git :
The '.git' directory is the heart of every Git repository. It contains all the files and metadata needed to track version history, branches, commits, and much more. Here's a description of the most important files and directories inside the '.git' directory:
1.   **HEAD**: This file points to the current branch. It usually contains a symbolic reference (a file path) to the 'refs/heads/branch_name' file which represents the active branch.
2.   **refs** : This directory contains sub-directories 'refs/heads', 'refs/tags', and 'refs/remotes' which respectively store pointers to local branches, tags, and remote branches (for remote repositories).
>   **refs/heads**: This directory contains one file for each local branch. Each file contains the SHA-1 of the last commit of this branch.
>   **refs/tags** : This directory stores tags, which are fixed points in the commit history to mark specific versions.
>   **refs/remotes** : If you are working with remote repositories, this directory contains references to remote branches, such as 'refs/remotes/origin/branch_name'.
3.   **objects** : This directory stores all Git objects, including commits, trees and blobs (the files themselves).
>   **objects/commit**: Contains the commits (each commit has a file with its SHA-1).
>   **objects/tree**: Contains trees, which are Git data structures that represent the state of the project at a given time.
>   **objects/blob**: Contains the blobs, which are the actual file data.
4.   **config**: This file contains the configuration of the Git repository, including user information (name, email address) and other repository-specific configuration settings.
5.   **description**: This file contains a short description of the repository, generally used by Git servers.
6.   **hooks** : This directory can contain hook scripts, which are scripts executed at specific times during Git operations (for example, before a commit).
7.   **index**: This file is the staging area. It contains information about the files that are ready to be committed in the next commit.
8.   **logs**: This directory can contain log files which record the history of references (for example, 'refs/heads/branch_name') and the operations performed on them.
9.   **info** : This directory may contain additional configuration and information files.
55. These files and directories form Git's internal infrastructure, which enables you to manage versions efficiently and track the history of commits to a project.

Step 4: Adding files and commits
1.   Create a **samplegit.py** file for your **RepProjectTest** project and type the following python code:

2. Add the file to the staging area

Before making a commit, we need to check that our project in the master branch contains no commits with the command

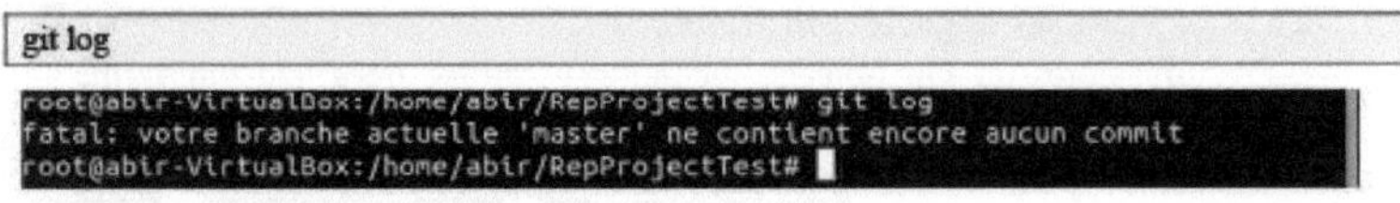

3.   Make a commit to save the changes:

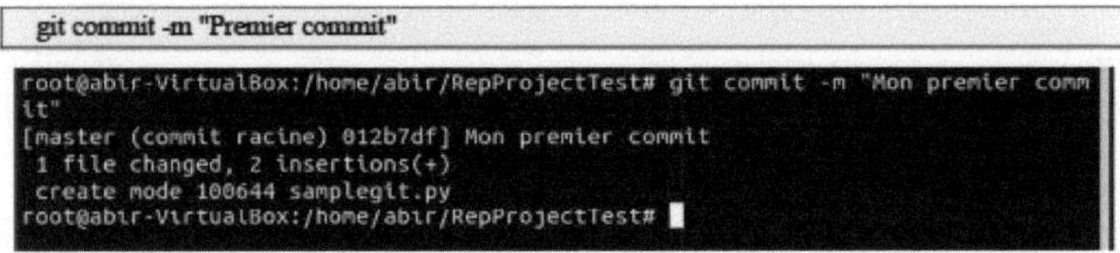

4.   View the commits history :

5.   Check the status of the master git status branch

6. Modify the **samplegit.py** file locally

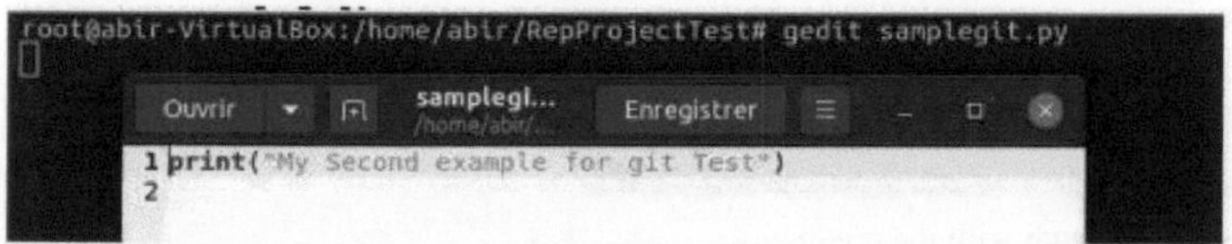

7. Now check the status of the git directory:

```
root@abir-VirtualBox:/home/abir/RepProjectTest# git status
Sur la branche master
Modifications qui ne seront pas validées :
  (utilisez "git add <fichier>..." pour mettre à jour ce qui sera validé)
  (utilisez "git restore <fichier>..." pour annuler les modifications dans le r
épertoire de travail)
        modifié :       samplegit.py

aucune modification n'a été ajoutée à la validation (utilisez "git add" ou "git
 commit -a")
```

We see that the **samplegit.py** ficmer is modified. In this case 2 cases are possible:

Case 1: We can restore it:

```
root@abir-VirtualBox:/home/abir/RepProjectTest# git restore samplegit.py
root@abir-VirtualBox:/home/abir/RepProjectTest# git status
Sur la branche master
rien à valider, la copie de travail est propre
root@abir-VirtualBox:/home/abir/RepProjectTest# cat samplegit.py
print("My first example for git Test")
```

Case 2: We can keep the modification and commit the new version

```
root@abir-VirtualBox:/home/abir/RepProjectTest# git  commit -a -m "Second Commi
t"
[master c297055] Second Commit
1 file changed, 1 insertion(+), 1 deletion(-)
```

8. Check the status of the master branch with the **git log** command

```
root@abir-VirtualBox:/home/abir/RepProjectTest# git  commit -a -m "Second Commi
t"
[master c297055] Second Commit
1 file changed, 1 insertion(+), 1 deletion(-)
root@abir-VirtualBox:/home/abir/RepProjectTest# git log
commit c297055646562da2dcb1abaa6fa9685383354f5d (HEAD -> master)
Author: Abir <abirakaldi@yahoo.fr>
Date:   Sun Oct 1 22:49:09 2023 +0100

    Second Commit

commit 012b7df94b16a7cfcc5eb6021223b79f79056716
Author: Abir <abirakaldi@yahoo.fr>
Date:   Sun Oct 1 22:28:18 2023 +0100

    Mon premier commit
```

9. Display the difference between the two versions of the commit with the command :

```
git diff id_commit1 id_commit2
```

```
root@abir-VirtualBox:/home/abir/RepProjectTest# git diff c297055646562da2dcb1ab
aa6fa9685383354f5d  012b7df94b16a7cfcc5eb6021223b79f79056716
diff --git a/samplegit.py b/samplegit.py
index a46fdcb..bf84224 100644
--- a/samplegit.py
+++ b/samplegit.py
@@ -1,2 +1,2 @@
-print("My second example for git Test")
+print("My first example for git Test")
```

Step 5: Creating branches

1. Creating a branch called developer git branch developer

```
git branch developer
```

```
root@abir-VirtualBox:/home/abir/RepProjectTest# git branch developer
```

2. Check that the branch has been created using the git branch command

```
git branch
```

```
root@abir-VirtualBox:/home/abir/RepProjectTest# git branch
  developer
* master
```

3.   Switch to the developer branch with the command

```
Git checkout developer
```

```
root@abir-VirtualBox:/home/abir/RepProjectTest# git checkout developer
Basculement sur la branche 'developer'
```

Step 6: Connecting Git with GitHub

1.   Create a GitHub account if you don't already have one.
2.   Connect to GitHub.
3.   Create a new GitHub repository called "RepGitTest" by following the steps on the platform.
4.   Associate the local repository with the "RepGitTest" GitHub repository using the following command (replace 'your_user' and 'your_project' with your information):

```
git remote add origin https://github.com/votre_utilisateur/RepProjectTest
```

```
root@abir-VirtualBox:/home/abir/RepProjectTest# git remote add origin https://g
ithub.com/AbirKaldi/RepProjectTest
```

5.   Push the local code to GitHub using the command :
git push -u origin master

```
git push -u origin master
```

```
root@abir-VirtualBox:/home/abir/RepProjectTest# git push origin master
Username for 'https://github.com': AbirKaldi
Password for 'https://AbirKaldi@github.com':
Énumération des objets: 12, fait.
Décompte des objets: 100% (12/12), fait.
Compression des objets: 100% (6/6), fait.
Écriture des objets: 100% (12/12), 1.02 Kio | 1.02 Mio/s, fait.
Total 12 (delta 0), réutilisés 0 (delta 0)
remote:
remote: Create a pull request for 'master' on GitHub by visiting:
remote:        https://github.com/AbirKaldi/RepProjectTest/pull/new/master
remote:
To https://github.com/AbirKaldi/RepProjectTest.git
 * [new branch]      master -> master
```

6.   You may need to authenticate with your GitHub username and token.
7.   Access the GitHub repository to check that your files have been successfully pushed.

## Chapter 3

Build tools

Introduction

Build tools are essential in the software dëvelopment cycle, as they automate the process of compiling, testing and dëploying applications. They allow source code to be transformed into an exëcutable version, while incorporating key ëtapes such as Гсхёсийпо automatedës testing, dëpendency management and package creation.

Popular tools such as Maven, Gradle and Ant are commonly used for Java projects, while Make is often used for C/C++ projects. These tools offer smooth, repeatable automation, ensuring that code is compiled in a consistent manner, thereby reducing the risk of human error.

Integrating build tools into a CI/CD pipeline also means that stable, valid versions of the software can be deployed more quickly.

Presentation of Maven

Maven is an open source tool from the Apache community, written entirely in Java. It automates the management and construction of a Java project: commonly known as a build tool.

Maven is presented as a command-line executable, but it is also natively integrated into the most common IDEs in the Java world: Eclipse, Intellij IDEA, NetBeans.

It is possible to create and run Java EE projects directly in IDEs. So why use Maven?

While an IDE may be sufficient to manage simple projects, this solution quickly proves to be limited:

S How can I share my project with other developers when they don't have exactly the same workstation configuration as me and don't use the same IDE as me?

S How can I compile and test my project outside an IDE (for example in a continuous integration process)?

S How can you automate certain repetitive tasks and reduce the number of errors or omissions?

The easiest way to solve all these problems is to use a tool like Maven.

Main features of Maven

❖ The most famous project construction tool is undoubtedly **make**. Make lets you define tasks with associated commands and dependencies between these tasks.

❖ Maven takes a very different approach: it divides the project build cycle into pre-defined phases and the developer can set or add tasks to be carried out automatically for each phase.

The main phases in Maven are :

compile: compilation of the project's source code

test: compilation of test source code and test execution

package: construction of the deliverable (for a Web application, this is the WAR archive)

■ Maven adds the possibility of automatically дёгег software dependencies. To dëvelop Java EE applications, we're going to need external libraries (.jar files in Java). Rather than going to tëlëcharge them one by one from the Web and adding them to Eclipse, we're going to tell Maven the identifier of the dëpendencies we need and it will take care of tëlëcharging them from a central repository, storing them in a cache on the machine and associating them with our project.

■ Finally, the Maven designers have adoptedë a normative approach in order to guarantee homogënëitë between projects. Thus a Maven project conforms to a fairly strict organisation of directories and files.

The Maven lifecycle

Maven is based on a multi-phase lifecycle structure to efficiently manage the construction and deployment of projects. The default lifecycle comprises three main cycles:

■ **Clean**: Cleans up the project by deleting files gënërës during previous compilations.

■ **Default (Build)**: This cycle contains most phases, from project validation to the дёпёгайоп of the final package. It includes ëtapes such as compilation (compile), ^xë^^ of tests (test), packaging (package), and dëploiement (deploy).

■ **Site**: Gënëre project documentation and reports in the form of a website.

Each phase of these cycles is exëcuted in a spëcific order, and dëvelopers can customise or add phases according to their needs. For example, to build and test a project, simply exëcute mvn clean install, which chains together all the necessary ëtapes ^.

Dependencies and the pom.xml file

Maven uses a central configuration file called pom.xml (Project Object Model) which defines the structure of the project and its dependencies. This file plays a key role in the automatic management of the external libraries that the project needs to function. Each dependency is defined by a set of attributes: **groupId**, **artifactId**, and **version**. Maven tëlë then automatically loads these libraries from remote dëp6ts such as Maven Central. Here's an example of dëpendency in a pom.xml file:

```
<dependency>
    <groupId>junit</groupId>
    <artifactId>junit</artifactId>
    <version>4.12</version>

    <scope>test</scope>
</dependency>
```

```
<scope>test</scope>
</dependency>
```

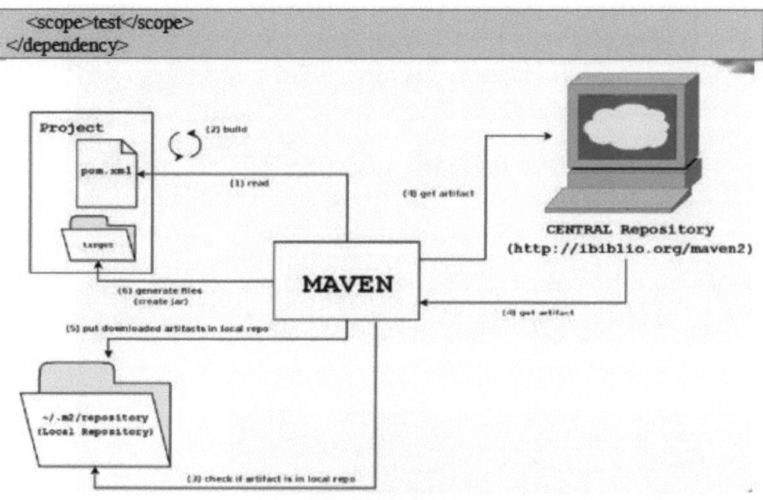

- Maven project -

Maven greatly simplifies dëpendency management by ëavoiding version conflicts and ensuring that the project always has the correct versions of the libraries.

Workshop 2. Setting up a Maven project

Step 1. Open a terminal on ubuntu and install maven with the command

```
apt-get install maven
```

```
root@Jenkins:/home/jenkins# apt-get install maven
Reading package lists... Done
Building dependency tree... Done
Reading state information... Done
maven is already the newest version (3.8.7-1).
The following packages were automatically installed and are no longer required
  java-wrappers jmeter-help libbatik-java libbcmail-java libbcpkix-java
  libbcprov-java libbcutil-java libbsf-java libbsh-java libcommons-codec-java
  libcommons-collections3-java libcommons-httpclient-java libcommons-jexl-java
  libcommons-jexl2-java libcommons-lang-java libcommons-math3-java
```

Step 2. Download and unzip the hello-webapp.zip archive.

```
wget https://gayerie.dev/epsi-poei-201705/assets/hello-webapp.zip
```

Unzip the hello-webapp.zip archive

```
root@Jenkins:/home/jenkins# unzip hello-webapp.zip
Archive:  hello-webapp.zip
   creating: hello/
 inflating: hello/pom.xml
   creating: hello/src/
   creating: hello/src/test/
   creating: hello/src/main/
   creating: hello/src/test/java/
   creating: hello/src/test/resources/
   creating: hello/src/main/java/
   creating: hello/src/main/resources/
   creating: hello/src/main/webapp/
   creating: hello/src/main/webapp/WEB-INF/
```

The archive will be decompressed in the hello directory. Access the hello directory and check its contents:

```
root@Jenkins:/home/jenkins# cd hello
root@Jenkins:/home/jenkins/hello# ls
pom.xml  src
root@Jenkins:/home/jenkins/hello# tree

├── pom.xml
    src
        main
            java
            resources
            webapp
                WEB-INF
                    web.xml
        test
            java
            resources
```

This archive contains the minimal Maven project for a Web application that we will use as an example.

Maven imposes a minimum file tree structure to ensure consistency across all projects.

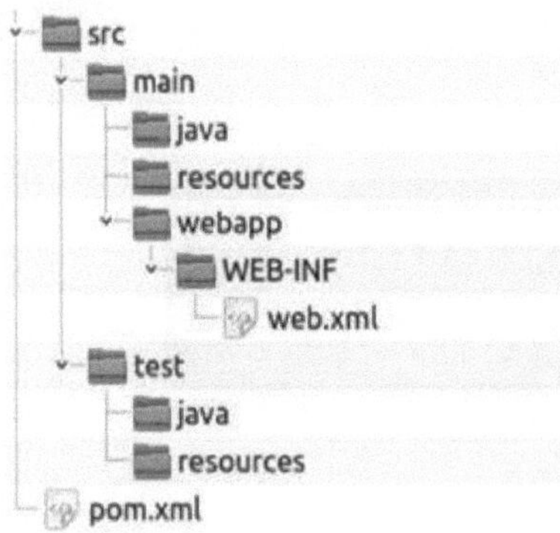

pom.xml
At the root of the project is the pom.xml file, the project descriptor for Maven.

src/main

This directory contains the application files. At least the **java** sub-directory contains the Java sources. The **resources** sub-directory contains files which are not Java sources but which must be present with the compiled files in the final application (these are often

configuration files). Finally, for a Web application, the **webapp** sub-directory corresponds to the root of the Web site. It contains the WEB-INF directory and the WEB-INF/web.xml file.

src/test

This directory contains the files used to test the application. The **Java** sub-directory contains the Java sources of the unit tests. The **resources** sub-directory contains files which are not Java sources but which are needed to run the tests (these are often configuration files for the tests).

There is one last directory to be aware of, the **target** directory. This directory is not present in the hello-webapp project tree. It is Maven's working directory. This directory is created automatically by Maven to store all the working files. It contains compiled classes, automatically generated source files, the final deliverable and test execution reports.

THE POM.XML FILE

The pom.xml file is the project descriptor for Maven. It is an XML file at the root of the project which is read by Maven to provide it with information about the project.

The contents of the pom.xml file for the hello-webapp project are as follows:

```xml
<project
    xmlns="http://maven.apache.org/POM/4.0.0" xmlns:xsi="http://www.w3.org/2001/XMLSchema-instance"
    xsi:schemaLocation="http://maven.apache.org/POM/4.0.0 http://maven.apache.org/xsd/maven-4.0.0.xsd">
    <!--
    La version du format du fichier pom.
    Actuellement la dernière version est la 4.0.0
    -->
    <modelVersion>4.0.0</modelVersion>

    <!--
    Le group ID de l'application. Le group ID
    s'apparente à un package Java mais pour un projet. Il évite
    une colision de nom dans le cas de deux projets ayant le même nom
    puisqu'ils peuvent avoir des group ID différents
    Ainsi si deux projets s'appelle hello et qu'ils ont des group ID
    différents, ils sont considérés comme étant des projets différents
    -->
    <groupId>fr.epsi.b3</groupId>

    <!--
    Le nom du projet
    -->
    <artifactId>hello</artifactId>

    <!--
    La version de notre projet. Maven gère le versionnage
    afin de permettre le suivi des évolutions d'un projet.
    Ici, le suffixe "-SNAPSHOT" indique à Maven que le projet
    est en cours de développement pour cette version.
    -->
    <version>0.0.1-SNAPSHOT</version>

    <!--
    Le type de packaging, c'est-à-dire le type de projet.
    Ici, on indique à Maven que le projet doit être package
    sous la forme d'un WAR. Donc pour Maven, il s'agit d'une
```

```xml
          application Web.
     -->
     <packaging>war</packaging>

     <!--
        Les propriétés de notre projet. On peut définir des propriétés
        spécifiques au projet ou des propriétés standard à Maven pour
        paramétrer la construction du projet.
     -->
     <properties>
        <!--
           Propriété standard définissant la version minimale de Java supportée
           par les fichiers sources (ici 1.8 pour Java 8)
        -->
        <maven.compiler.source>1.8</maven.compiler.source>

        <!--
           Propriété standard définissant la version Java des fichiers compilés
           du projet (ici 1.8 pour Java 8)
        -->
        <maven.compiler.target>1.8</maven.compiler.target>

        <!--
           Le format d'encodage des fichiers source du projet. Attention, l'encodage
           par défaut n'est pas le même sous Windows et sous les systèmes *NIX.
           Il est donc plus sage de toujours positionner cette propriété dans le fichier pom.xml
        -->
        <project.build.sourceEncoding>UTF-8</project.build.sourceEncoding>
     </properties>
</project>
```

This pom.xml file provides Maven with the minimum information:

- The project is called en.epsi.b3:hello
- The current version is 0.0.1 and is a working version.
- The project is a Java EE Web application (war)
- The project is written in Java 8 and the sources are encoded in UTF-8 ■

MANAGING THE PROJECT WITH MAVEN

You can use the mvn command line from the directory containing the **pom.xml** file to perform operations on a project. Maven creates a working directory called **target** in which it stores the files produced (including war files).

Step 3. Clean up the **target** working directory

```
root@Jenkins:/home/jenkins/hello# mvn clean
[INFO] Scanning for projects...
[INFO]
[INFO] -----------------------< fr.epsi.b3:hello >-----------------------
[INFO] Building hello 0.0.1-SNAPSHOT
[INFO] --------------------------------[ war ]---------------------------
Downloading from central: https://repo.maven.apache.org/maven2/org/apache/maven/
plugins/maven-clean-plugin/2.5/maven-clean-plugin-2.5.pom
Downloaded from central: https://repo.maven.apache.org/maven2/org/apache/maven/p
lugins/maven-clean-plugin/2.5/maven-clean-plugin-2.5.pom (3.9 kB at 3.2 kB/s)
Downloading from central: https://repo.maven.apache.org/maven2/org/apache/maven/
plugins/maven-plugins/22/maven-plugins-22.pom
Downloaded from central: https://repo.maven.apache.org/maven2/org/apache/maven/p
```

At the end of this phase, the display will look like this:

```
s/plexus-utils/3.0/plexus-utils-3.0.jar (226 kB at 683 kB/s)
[INFO] -----------------------------------------------------------------
[INFO] BUILD SUCCESS
[INFO] -----------------------------------------------------------------
[INFO] Total time:  5.057 s
[INFO] Finished at: 2024-04-23T11:14:01+01:00
[INFO] -----------------------------------------------------------------
root@Jenkins:/home/jenkins/hello#
```

Step 4. Compile the sources

mvn compile)

compile sources, unit tests and run unit tests

```
root@Jenkins:/home/jenkins/hello# mvn compile
[INFO] Scanning for projects...
[INFO]
[INFO] -----------------------< fr.epsi.b3:hello >-----------------------
[INFO] Building hello 0.0.1-SNAPSHOT
[INFO] --------------------------------[ war ]--------------------------------
[INFO]
[INFO] --- maven-resources-plugin:2.6:resources (default-resources) @ hello ---
[INFO] Using 'UTF-8' encoding to copy filtered resources.
[INFO] Copying 0 resource
[INFO]
[INFO] --- maven-compiler-plugin:3.1:compile (default-compile) @ hello ---
[INFO] Nothing to compile - all classes are up to date
[INFO]
[INFO] BUILD SUCCESS
[INFO]
[INFO] Total time:  1.215 s
[INFO] Finished at: 2024-04-23T11:19:14+01:00
[INFO]
root@Jenkins:/home/jenkins/hello# mvn compile
[INFO] Scanning for projects...
[INFO]
[INFO] -----------------------< fr.epsi.b3:hello >-----------------------
[INFO] Building hello 0.0.1-SNAPSHOT
[INFO] --------------------------------[ war ]--------------------------------
[INFO]
[INFO] --- maven-resources-plugin:2.6:resources (default-resources) @ hello ---
[INFO] Using 'UTF-8' encoding to copy filtered resources.
[INFO] Copying 0 resource
[INFO]
[INFO] --- maven-compiler-plugin:3.1:compile (default-compile) @ hello ---
```

Step 5. Now test the build

`mvn test`

```
root@Jenkins:/home/jenkins/hello# mvn test
[INFO] Scanning for projects...
[INFO]
[INFO] -----------------------< fr.epsi.b3:hello >-----------------------
[INFO] Building hello 0.0.1-SNAPSHOT
[INFO] --------------------------------[ war ]--------------------------------
Downloading from central: https://repo.maven.apache.org/maven2/org/apache/maven/plugin
ven-surefire-plugin-2.12.4.pom
Downloaded from central: https://repo.maven.apache.org/maven2/org/apache/maven/plugins
```

At the end of this task we have the following result:

```
[INFO] --------------------------------------------------------
[INFO] BUILD SUCCESS
[INFO] --------------------------------------------------------
[INFO] Total time:  5.721 s
[INFO] Finished at: 2024-04-23T11:21:04+01:00
[INFO] --------------------------------------------------------
```

Step 6. Now dëployer the package: compile the sources, unit tests, exëcute the unit tests and create the war file.

`mvn package`

```
root@Jenkins:/home/jenkins/hello# mvn package
[INFO] Scanning for projects...
[INFO]
[INFO] -----------------------< fr.epsi.b3:hello >-----------------------
[INFO] Building hello 0.0.1-SNAPSHOT
[INFO] --------------------------------[ war ]--------------------------------
Downloading from central: https://repo.maven.apache.org/maven2/org/apache/maven/plugins/mave
plugin-2.2.pom
Downloading from central: https://repo.maven.apache.org/maven2/org/apache/maven/plugins/maven
lugin-2.2.pom (6.5 kB at 11 kB/s)
Downloading from central: https://repo.maven.apache.org/maven2/org/apache/maven/plugins/mave
```

At the end of this phase we have the following result:

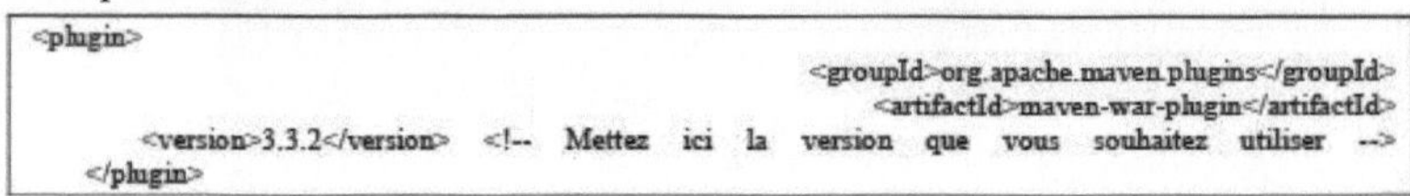

NB: If you encounter a problem with the mvn package command, add the following plugin
to the pom.xml file:

```xml
<plugin>
    <groupId>org.apache.maven.plugins</groupId>
    <artifactId>maven-war-plugin</artifactId>
    <version>3.3.2</version> <!-- Mettez ici la version que vous souhaitez utiliser -->
</plugin>
```

The pom.xml file then looks like this

```xml
1 <project xmlns="http://maven.apache.org/POM/4.0.0" xmlns:xsi="http://www.w3.org/2001/
  XMLSchema-instance"
2         xsi:schemaLocation="http://maven.apache.org/POM/4.0.0 http://maven.apache.org/
  xsd/maven-4.0.0.xsd">
3         <modelVersion>4.0.0</modelVersion>
4         <groupId>fr.epsi.b3</groupId>
5         <artifactId>hello</artifactId>
6         <version>0.0.1-SNAPSHOT</version>
7         <packaging>war</packaging>
8         <properties>
9             <maven.compiler.source>1.8</maven.compiler.source>
10            <maven.compiler.target>1.8</maven.compiler.target>
11            <project.build.sourceEncoding>UTF-8</project.build.sourceEncoding>
12        </properties>
13        <build>
14    <plugins>
15        <plugin>
16            <groupId>org.apache.maven.plugins</groupId>
17            <artifactId>maven-war-plugin</artifactId>
18            <version>3.3.2</version> <!-- Mettez ici la version que vous souhaitez
  utiliser -->
19        </plugin>
20        <!-- Autres plugins -->
21    </plugins>
22 </build>
23 </project>
```

Step 7: Adding the TOMEE plugin to the pom.xml file

We're going to run a tomEE server directly from Maven

You can declare plugins in a pom.xml file in your project. There are many plugins available
from Maven repositories. This means that declaring a plugin automatically triggers its
download, installation and execution.

When creating a project for a Web application, it can be useful to be able to run it from
Maven, i.e. to launch a Java EE application server and deploy the application to this server.
. For TomEE, you can use the tomee-maven-plugin. Go back to the Maven project and edit the
pom.xml file to add the tomee plugin:

```xml
<build>
  <plugins>
   <plugin>
    <!-- le plugin pour démarrer TomEE depuis la ligne de commande avec maven :
      mvn package tomee:run
    -->
    <groupId>org.apache.tomee.maven</groupId>
    <artifactId>tomee-maven-plugin</artifactId>
    <version>8.0.9</version>
    <configuration>
     <tomeeVersion>8.0.9</tomeeVersion>
     <tomeeClassifier>plus</tomeeClassifier>
    </configuration>
   </plugin>
  </plugins>
</build>
```

Step 8. Open a terminal and go to your project directory. Type the command :

```
mvn package tomee:run
```

package tells Maven that it must build the project, run the unit tests and create the package (in our case a war file). Then tomee:run directly calls the tomee-maven- plugin and asks it to launch the server by deploying the war cred file.

The tomee-maven-plugin plugin deploys the application in the [artifact-id]-[version] root context. For the test project, the ddploiement context will therefore be **hello-0.0.1-SNAPSHOT**

```
23-Apr-2024 12:15:14.397 INFO [main] jdk.internal.reflect.DelegatingMethodAccessorImpl.invoke Deployment of web applica
tion archive [/home/jenkins/hello/target/apache-tomee/webapps/hello-0.0.1-SNAPSHOT.war] has finished in [9.591] ms
23-Apr-2024 12:15:14.400 INFO [main] jdk.internal.reflect.DelegatingMethodAccessorImpl.invoke Starting ProtocolHandler
["http-nio-8080"]
```

## Chapter 4

Docker

Docker: Concepts and use

Docker allows you to create containers, lightweight units containing an application and all its dependencies, to make it portable and consistent in different environments. Docker solves the problem of "it works on my machine" by providing a coherent, isolated environment for each application.
Example:

You have a Node.js application that works in development but encounters problems in production because of configuration differences. With Docker, you encapsulate the application in a container, ensuring that it runs identically everywhere.

Docker architecture

Docker is made up of several main components, which work together to enable containers and images to be managed. These components include Docker Engine, containers, images, volumes, networks and registries.

*   Docker Engine

The Docker Engine is the heart of the Docker ecosystem. It is made up of several key elements:

o Docker Daemon: The daemon that manages the creation and execution of containers.

It receives commands from the user interface and interacts with file systems, networks and containers.

o Docker CLI: The command line interface used to communicate with the Docker daemon. For example, when you run 'docker run', the command is sent to the Docker daemon for execution.

o REST API: A set of APIs that allow external tools to communicate with Docker, for example via scripts or third-party applications.

*   Docker images

A Docker image is a kind of template used to create containers. Each image contains everything an application needs to run: the application code, libraries, dependencies and even the operating system, all encapsulated in a single image.

Docker images are built in layers, with each instruction in a Dockerfile creating a new layer. This means that parts of the image can be reused in other projects to save space and speed up the build process.

*   Containers

Containers are instances of Docker images. Once the image has been built, the container is the running instance. Containers are isolated from other containers and the host, but they can share networks and volumes to enable communication and data persistence.

Containers operate in isolated and independent environments. They have their own process space, network and file system.

By default, containers are ephemeral, meaning that the data they contain is deleted once they are stopped, unless they use volumes to persist the data.

*   Docker volumes

Volumes are storage spaces shared between the host and the containers to persist data beyond the lifetime of the container. They can also be used to share data between different containers.
Example:

```
docker run -v /path/on/host:/path/in/container my-python-app
```

In this example, '/path/on/host' is the directory on the host, and '/path/in/container' is the location in the container where this volume will be mounted.

*   Docker networks

Docker lets you create virtual networks so that containers can communicate with each other or with the outside world. Network types include :

S Bridge: Containers in a bridge network can talk to each other.

S Host: The container shares the host network.

S Overlay: Allows containers on different Docker hosts to connect.

Example

docker network create my-network

docker run --network my-network my-container

Here, a custom Docker network is created and the container is attached to this network.

- Docker registries

A registry is a repository where Docker images are stored. The most commonly used public registry is Docker Hub, but companies can also set up private registries to store their images.

Example of pushing an image onto Docker Hub:

docker tag my-image username/my-image

docker push username/my-image

Docker Images: Construction, Optimisation and Management

Docker images are snapshots containing everything needed to run an application. They are built from a Dockerfile and optimised to reduce their size and deployment time.

Example of a Dockerfile :

For a Python application, you can create a Docker image with this Dockerfile :

FROM python:3.9-slim

\# Copy the source code into the COPY . /app container

\# WORKDIR /app directory definition

\# Installing dependencies using pip RUN pip install -r requirements.txt

\# Port 5000 exposure for Flask EXPOSE 5000

\# Command to start CMD application ["python", "app.py"]

Docker Container Management: Manipulation and Orchestration

Containers are the active instances of images. Once the image is ready, you can launch it with 'docker run', manage the volumes, and configure the networks between several containers.

Example:

To launch a container from the previously created image :

```
docker run -d -p 5000:5000 my-python-app
```

Dockerfile: Image construction and optimisation

The Dockerfile is a text file describing how Docker should build an image. It is essential to optimise this file to reduce the size of images and speed up the build process.

Example of an optimised Dockerfile for a Python :

\# Use of the official Python image

FROM python:3.9-slim

\# Installing system dependencies

RUN apt-get update && apt-get install -y \

libpq-dev gcc

\# Creating a non-root user

RUN useradd -ms /bin/bash appuser

\# User definition

USER appuser

\# Copy of source code

WORKDIR /app

COPY --chown=appuser:appuser . /app

\# Installing Python dependencies

RUN pip install --no-cache-dir -r requirements.txt

```
#    Port exhibition for Flask
EXHIBITION 5000
#    Command to start the application
CMD ["python", "app.py"]
```

Docker Compose: Simplifying Multi-Container Environments

Docker Compose lets you manage several containers using a YAML configuration file.

Example of docker-compose.yml :

```
version: "3"
services:
web:
image: node:14
working_dir: /app
volumes:
-    .:/app
ports:
-    "3000:3000"
command: npm start
depends_on:
- mongo
mongo:
image: mongo:4.4
ports:
-    "27017:27017"
volumes:
-    mongo-data:/data/db
volumes:
mongo-data:
```

Docker integration with CI/CD

Docker integrates perfectly into CI/CD pipelines to automate the creation, testing and deployment of applications.

Example with Jenkins :

```
pipeline {
agent {
docker {
image 'node:14'
}
}
courses {
stage('Build') {
steps {
sh 'npm install'
}
}
stage('Test') {
steps {
sh 'npm test'
}
}
stage('Deploy') {
```

```
steps {
sh 'docker build -t my-app .'
sh 'docker run -d -p 3000:3000 my-app'
}
}
}
}
```

Docker security: best practices and tools

Security is a critical aspect when using Docker, especially when containers are deployed in production. Although Docker provides isolation between containers and the host, there are security risks associated with configuring images, containers and the network. This section covers best practices for securing Docker environments, as well as useful tools for analysing and strengthening the security of deployments.

Secure Docker Images

1. Use official or verified images: When choosing images for your containers, give preference to those from official sources or verified on Docker Hub or a secure private registry. This will minimise the risk of malware or compromised images being executed.

- Example: Rather than using an unknown image such as 'node:random', use the official image 'node: 14' or images with specific tags to control versions.

FROM node: 14

2. Update your images regularly: Security vulnerabilities may exist in the base images or in the dependencies included in the image. It is important to regularly update your images and rebuild your containers to include the latest patches.

- Example: If you use a Python image, make sure you always use an updated version to avoid known security flaws.

```
FROM python :3.10 -slim
```

3. Minimise image size: The smaller your image, the fewer potentially vulnerable dependencies it contains. Use "slim" or "alpine" images, which are minimal versions of an operating system or runtime.

- Example: Use 'node:alpine' instead of 'node' for a lighter version.

```
FROM node: 14-alpine
```

Securing containers

1. Avoid running containers as root: By default, Docker containers run with root privileges, which can pose a significant security risk if the container is compromised. Use a non-root user to run processes in the container.

\# Example: Create a non-root user in your Dockerfile and define it as the default user.

\# Create an 'appuser' user

RUN useradd -ms /bin/bash appuser

\# Change the default user

USER appuser

2. Use namespaces for isolation: Docker uses Linux namespaces to isolate container processes, networks and file systems from each other and from the host. Enabling user namespaces reinforces this isolation by mapping container UIDs and GIDs to non-root users on the host.

3. Limit container resources: Use options such as '--memory' and '--cpus' to limit the system resources that a container can consume. This reduces the risk of a malicious or faulty container draining host resources.

- Example: Limit memory and CPU usage for a container.

```
docker run -d --memory="512m" --cpus="1.5" my-python-app
```

4.   Privilege management: Use the '--cap-drop' option to remove unnecessary Linux capabilities from the container. By default, Docker grants several capabilities to the container. You can reduce these capabilities to limit what the container can do.
- Example: Delete all capacities and add only those you need.
docker run --cap-drop=ALL --cap-add=NET_ADMIN my-container

Securing the Docker network
1. Use custom networks: Docker containers are by default connected to the "bridge" network, which allows them to communicate with other containers on the same machine. Create custom networks to isolate your containers and limit their range.
- Example: Create a custom network and attach containers to this network.

```
docker network create --driver bridge my-secure-network
docker run --network my-secure-network my-secure-container
```

- Enable firewalls: Use firewall rules to control incoming and outgoing connections to your containers. For example, with 'iptables', you can restrict connections to certain ports only.

3. Isolating ports: Do not publish ports that are not needed externally. Only expose the ports you need for the application using the ' -p' option.
- Example: If you only need port 8080 for a web application, don't expose any other ports.
docker run -d -p 8080:8080 my-web-app

Docker Security Tools
1.   Docker Bench for Security: An open-source script that checks your Docker installation for compliance with security best practices. It analyses various aspects of Docker configuration, including container configuration, networks and permissions.
- Example: Run Docker Bench for Security to audit your Docker installation.

```
git clone https://github.com/docker/docker-bench-security.git
cd docker-bench-security
sh docker-bench-security.sh
```

2.   Trivy: An open-source scanner that detects vulnerabilities in Docker images, as well as in Kubernetes, Terraform and Docker Compose configuration files.
- Example: Run a Trivy scan to check for vulnerabilities in a Docker image.
trivy image my-docker-image

3.   Clair : Another vulnerability scanning tool for Docker images. It scans images and provides a detailed report of the security holes present.

4.   Notary: Docker also includes a content signing feature called Notary. This allows you to cryptographically sign your images to ensure that they have not been altered between creation and deployment.
- Example: Use Docker Content Trust to sign an image before pushing it onto a registry.
export DOCKER_CONTENT_TRUST=1
docker push myrepo/myimage:mytag

Best Deployment Practices
1.   **Monitor containers in real time**: Use tools such as **Falco** to monitor suspicious activity at container level in real time. This allows you to detect abnormal behaviour such as unauthorised access to sensitive files or kernel modifications.

2.   Automate updates: Make sure that your containers and images are regularly updated with the latest secure versions. Use continuous deployment (CI/CD) systems to automate this process.

3.   Scan images before deployment: Integrate security tools such as Trivy and Clair into your CI/CD pipelines to scan images before pushing them into production. This makes it possible to block any deployments containing critical vulnerabilities.

Workshop 3. Docker

Part 1: Basic Docker commands

1. Installing Docker

sudo apt install docker.io

2. Starting the Docker service sudo systemctl start docker
3. Verifying the installation of Docker docker --version
4. List Docker docker images
5. List containers currently running docker ps
6. Creating an interactive container

docker run -it ubuntu /bin/bash

7. Starting a container in the background docker run -d nginx
8. Execute a command in a running container docker exec -it container_id /bin/bash
9. Stopping a running container docker stop container_id
10. Delete a container stops docker rm container_id

Part 2: Creating an image from a container

1. Creating a basic container

```
docker run -d --name my-container ubuntu
```

2. Customise the container

```
docker exec -it my-container /bin/bash
```

3. Create an image from the custom container** docker commit my-container my-image:v1
4. List images to check the new image** docker images
5. Delete the docker container stop my-container docker rm my-container
6. Run a base container on the new docker image run -it my-image:v1 /bin/bash
7. Make changes to the base container on the image and install python in the container apt-get install python3
8. Create a new version of the docker image commit my-container my-image:v2
9. **List images to check the new version** docker images
10. Delete the container based on the old image docker stop my-image:v1 docker rm my-image:v1

Part 3: Using docker build

For this section, we're going to use a concrete example by creating a Docker image for a customised Nginx web server.

1. Creating a directory for your project

mkdir my_project_nginx

cd my_project_nginx

2. Creating a Dockerfile

```
gedit Dockerfile
```

This file will contain the instructions for building the Docker image.

```
# Use an Nginx base image
FROM nginx:latest
# Copy a custom configuration file into the container
COPY nginx.conf /etc/nginx/nginx.conf
```

3. Creating a custom Nginx configuration file

Create a custom Nginx configuration file called "nginx.conf" in the same directory as your Dockerfile with the desired configurations.

Example of a custom Nginx configuration

server {

listen 80;

server_name example.com;

location / {
root /usr/share/nginx/html;
index index.html;
}
}
4.   Building an image from the Dockerfile
Use the following command to build an image from the Dockerfile located in the current directory:

```
docker build -t my-nginx-personalise:1.0 .
```

5.   List images to check the new image

```
docker images
```

6.   Run a base container on the constructed image

```
docker run -d -p 8080:80 mon-nginx-personnalise:1.0
```

7.   Checking container execution
Open a web browser and go to **'http://localhost:8080'** to see if Nginx works with your customised configuration.
8.   Stop and delete the container
docker stop container_id
docker rm container_id
9.   Clean up unused containers and images
To clean up unused containers and images, run the following commands: docker container prune
docker image prune
10.   Delete local image

```
docker rmi my-nginx-customized: 1.0
```

Part 4: Using Docker Compose
For this part, we're going to use a concrete example by creating a Docker Compose environment for a Python web application based on Flask and a MySQL database server. Make sure you have Docker Compose installed on your system.
Docker installation compose :

```
sudo apt install docker-compose
```

1.   Creating a directory for your project
mkdir my_project_flask
cd my_project_flask
2.   Create a 'docker-compose.yml' file
Create a 'docker-compose.yml' file in the project directory. This file will define the configuration of your application and contains the following instructions:
version: '3'
services:
web:
image: python:3.8-slim
command: python app.py
volumes:
-    ./app:/app
ports:
-    5000:5000
db:
image: mysql:5.7
environment:
MYSQL_ROOT_PASSWORD: my-secret-pw

MYSQL_DATABASE: mydb
MYSQL_USER: myuser
MYSQL_PASSWORD: mypassword

3.   Creating an 'app' directory for your Flask application

```
mkdir app
```

4.   Create an 'app.py' file for your Flask application

Create an 'app.py' file in the 'app' directory with your Flask code.

```
from flask import Flask
```

```
import mysql.connector app = Flask(    name   )
@app.route('/') def hello():
return 'Hello, World!'    ifname==        '        main_
app.run(host='0.0.0.0')
```

5.   Running 1 application with Docker Compose

In your project's main directory, run the following command to start the services defined in the 'docker-compose.yml' file:

```
docker-compose up -d
```

6.   Checking the Flask application

Open a web browser and go to 'http://localhost:5000' to check that your Flask application is running.

7.   Stop Docker Compose services

To stop the services, run the following command in your project's main directory:

```
docker-compose down
```

8.   Delete Docker Compose containers and volumes

If you want to completely delete the containers and volumes created by Docker Compose, use the following command :

```
docker-compose down -v
```

Part 5: Deploying a Python application with Docker

In this part, we will deploy a simple Python Flask application using a real Python image using Docker Compose. Follow these 10 steps to accomplish this task:

1.   Creating a directory for your project

Create a dedicated directory for your Docker project:

```
mkdir my_python_project
cd my_python_project
```

2.   Creating a Dockerfile

Create a Dockerfile in your project directory. This file will contain instructions for building the Docker image for your Python Flask application.

```
gedit Dockerfile
```

```
#     Use a Python base image
```

```
FROM python:3.8-slim
#     Define the working directory in the WORKDIR /app container
#     Copy the Python dependencies file COPY requirements.txt .
#     Install the Python dependencies
RUN pip install --no-cache-dir -r requirements.txt
#     Copy the source code into the COPY .
#     Default command to run the CMD application ["python", "app.py"].
```

3.   Create a ' requirements .txt' file

Create a 'requirements.txt' file to list the dependencies of your Python Flask application. For example :

flask=2.0.1

4.   Create an 'app' directory for your Python application mkdir app

5.   Create an 'app.py' file for your Python Flask application

Create an 'app.py' file in the 'app' directory with your Flask Python code. Here is a simple example

from flask import Flask app = Flask(name   )

@app.route('/') def hello():

return 'Hello, World!'   ifname==   '   main   ':

app.run(host='0.0.0.0')

6.   Create a 'docker-compose.yml' file

Create a 'docker-compose.yml' file in the main directory of your project to define the configuration of your application and associated services.

version: '3'

services:

aPP:

build:

context: .

dockerfile: Dockerfile

ports:

- 5000:5000

7.   Building the Docker image

Run the following command to build the Docker image from the Dockerfile: docker-compose build

8.   Running the application with Docker Compose

Start the application by running the service defined in the 'docker-compose.yml' file: docker-compose up -d

9.   Checking the Flask application

Open a web browser and access ' http://localhost: 5000' to check that your Python Flask application is working correctly.

10.   Stopping and cleaning Docker Compose containers

To stop Docker Compose services, run the following command in your project's main directory:

```
docker-compose down
```

If you also want to completely delete the containers and volumes created by Docker Compose, use the following command :

```
docker-compose down -v
```

## Chapter 5

CI/CD pipeline with Jenkins

Introducing Jenkins

❖ Dedicated to DevOps, Jenkins is an open source continuous integration tool (under MIT licence) developed in Java.

❖ Each time an application's code is modified in the configuration manager, Jenkins automatically recompiles and tests it.

❖ For this second stage, Jenkins integrates the JUnit open source test framework. If an error is detected, Jenkins alerts the developer so that he can resolve the problem.

❖ This is obviously a highly advantageous process for a development project.

❖ Fork of the Hudson tool, Jenkins is backed by a servlet server such as Apache Tomcat or can be based on its own embedded web server.

❖ Accessible via a web browser, it is compatible with the most popular version management systems such as Git and Subversion. As standard, it supports continuous integration (CI) pipelines based on the Apache Ant and Apache Maven build tools.

Jenkins plugins

Through its Update Center, Jenkins offers 1,500 plugins for extending its continuous integration environment. Among the most popular are :

S **Dashboard View Plugin** for monitoring the status of tasks,

S **Monitoring Plugin** that measures job performance,

S **Kubernetes Plugin** that manages the deployment of Jenkins agents on a Kubernetes infrastructure,

S **Multijob Plugin** which is sized to orchestrate the execution of complex tasks sequentially,

S **GitHub API** that schedules and starts builds based on code extracted from GitHub,

S **Git Client** provides a Git API for Jenkins plugins.

Types of Jenkins pipelines

Jenkins pipelines are workflows that can be **complex, describing all the stages in a continuous integration process**. These pipelines **are declared in files** called **Jenkinsfiles**.

JenkinsFiles can be **written** using **two types of syntax** based on the **Groovy DSL**:

1. **Pipeline Declarative :**

The declarative pipeline is a simplified and structured way of defining pipelines in Jenkins using predefined directives.

```groovy
pipeline {
    agent any
    stages {
        stage('Build') {
            steps {
                // Étapes de construction (compilation, tests...)
                echo 'Building...'
            }
        }
        stage('Test') {
            steps {
                // Étapes de test
                echo 'Testing...'
            }
        }
        stage('Deploy') {
            steps {
                // Étapes de déploiement
                echo 'Deploying...'
            }
        }
    }
}
```

Pipeline Description :

The script pipeline uses a complete Groovy script to define the pipeline. Here is an example:

```groovy
node {
    stage('Build') {
        // Étapes de construction
        echo 'Building...'
    }
    stage('Test') {
        // Étapes de test
        echo 'Testing...'
    }
    stage('Deploy') {
        // Étapes de déploiement
        echo 'Deploying...'
    }
}
```

Jenkins architecture

S Jenkins uses **a master/agent** architecture.

Jenkins master contains all its configurations. The **master orchestrates** and **controls the execution** of all the **workflows** defined in **pipelines** and executed on **agent nodes**. There are two types of newel: **static agents** and **dynamic** agents (provisioned as required).

S **Static na'iids** are installed on VMs directly, whereas **dynamic na'iids are provisioned** on **kubernetes clusters** or in **containers**. The **master** can also be installed on a **kubernetes cluster**.

S To communicate with agents, the master uses either the **SSH protocol**, the **JNLP protocol** (port 5000) or **API calls**.

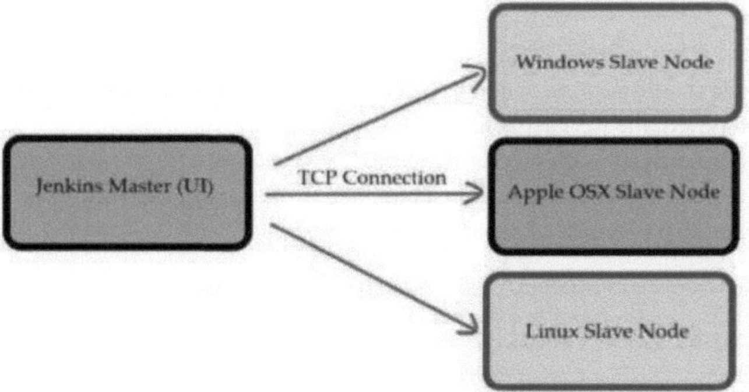

Architecture of a Jenkins cluster

Workshop 4. Setting up a CI/CD pipeline with Jenkins

Part 1. Preparing the working environment

Step 1: Open the terminal and rёcиpёгег the sample-app directory from github with the command :

git clone http://github.com/AbirKaldi/sample-app

Step 2: Dёplacer the sample-app directory in your own github account.

Part 2. Download and run the Jenkins Docker image

In this part, you will tёlёload the Jenkins Docker image.You will then dёmarket an instance of the image and vёverify that the Jenkins server is running exёcution.

Step 1. Tёlёload the Jenkins Docker image

The Jenkins Docker image is stockёe here: https://hub.docker.com/r/jenkins/jenkins.Au at the time of writing this lab, this spёcifies that you use the docker pull jenkins/jenkins command to tёlёload the latest Jenkins container.You should get a result similar to the following:

devasc@labvm:~# **docker pull jenkins/jenkins:lts** lts: Pulling from jenkins/jenkins 3192219afd04: Pulling fs layer 17c160265e75: Pulling fs layer cc4fe40d0e61: Pulling fs layer 9d647f502a07: Pulling fs layer d108b8c498aa: Pulling fs layer 1bfe918b8aa5: Pulling complete dafa1a7c0751: Pulling complete 650a236d0150: Pull complete cba44e30780e: Pull complete 52e2f7d12a4d: Pull complete d642af5920ea: Pull complete e65796f9919e: Pull complete 9138dabbc5cc: Pull complete f6289c08656c: Pull complete 73d6b450f95c: Pull complete a8f96fbec6a5: Pull complete 9b49ca1b4e3f: Pull complete d9c8f6503715: Pull complete 20fe25b7b8af: Pull complete

Digest: sha256:717dcbe5920753187a20ba43058ffd3d87647fa903d98cde64dda4f4c82c5c48 Status: Downloaded newer image for jenkins/jenkins :lts docker.io/j enkins/j enkins:lts

devasc@labvm:~/labs/devnet-src/jenkins/sample-app$

Step 2. Dёmarry the Jenkins Docker container.Enter the following one-line command.You may need to copy it into a ёtext editor if you are viewing a PDF version of this lab to ёavoid line breaks.This command will dёmarry the Jenkins Docker container, then allow Гcxёcийcп Docker commands inside your Jenkins server.

devasc@labvm:~/labs/devnet-src/jenkins/sample-app$ **docker run --rm -u root -p 8080:8080 -v jenkins-data:/var/jenkins_home -v $(which docker):　　　/usr/bin/docker-v /var/run/docker.sock:/var/run/docker.sock -v "$HOME":/home --name jenkins_server jenkins/jenkins:lts** The useful options in this **docker run** command are as follows:

o **-rm** - This option automatically deletes the Docker container when you stop exёcuting it.

o **-u** - This option spёcifies the user. You want this Docker container to exёcute as root so that all Docker commands entered into the Jenkins server are autorisёes.

o **-p** - This option spёcifies the port on which the Jenkins server will exёcut locally.

o **-v** - These options link the rkcessary mount volumes for Jenkins and Docker. The first **-v** spёcifies where Jenkins domkes will be stockёes. The second **-v** spёcifies or get Docker so you can exёcute Docker in the

Docker container that exëcutes the Jenkins server. The third **-v** spëcifies the PATH variable for the base directory.

Step 3. VC'rinez that the Jenkins server is running ^xĕ^й^.

The Jenkins server should now be running ^xĕ^от. Copy the admin password that appears in the output, as indiqire in the next section.

Do not enter any commands in this server window. If you accidentally stop the Jenkins server, you will need to re-enter the docker run command from step 2 above. After the initial installation, the admin password is displayed as shown below.

```
<output omitted>
Jenkins initial setup is required.An admin user has been created and a password generated.
Please use the following password to proceed to installation:
77dc402e31324c1b917f230af7bfebf2<--Your password will be different
This may also be found at: /var/jenkins_home/secrets/initialAdminPassword
<output omitted>
2020-05-12 16:34:29.608+0000 [id=19] INFO hudson.WebAppMain$3#run: Jenkins is fully up and running
```

Note: If you lose the password, or it does not display as indiqik above, or you need to reëstart the Jenkins server, you can still rëcupërer the password by helping at the command line of the Jenkins Docker container. Create a second terminal window in VS Code and enter the following commands so as not to stop the Jenkins server...:

devasc@labvm:~ # **docker exec -it jenkins_server /bin/bash**

root@19d2a847a54e:/# **cat /var/jenkins_home/secrets/initialAdminPassword**

77dc402e31324c1b917f230af7bfebf2

root@19d2a847a54e:/# **exit** exit

devasc@labvm:~/labs/devnet-src/jenkins/sample-app$

Note: Your container ID (19d2a847a54e highlighted above) and password will be different.

Step 4. Study the abstraction levels currently running on your computer.

The following ASCII diagram shows the levels of abstraction in this Docker Inside-Docker (dind) implementation, a level of complexity not uncommon in today's networks and cloud infrastructures.

```
       ++
|Your Computer's Operating System | ++          |
|DEVASC VM | |
| | ++ | |
| |Docker container | | |
| | | ++    | | |
| | | Jenkins server | | | | Jenkins server
| | | | ++   | | | |
| | |Docker container| | | | |
| | | | ++   | | | |
| | | ++    | | |
| | ++ | |
| ++  |
       ++
```

Part 3. Configuring Jenkins

In this section, you will complete the initial configuration of the Jenkins server.

Step 1: Open a web browser tab.

Go **to http://localhost:8080/** and log in using your copy password.

Step 2. Install the recommended Jenkins plugins.

Click on **Install suggested plugins** and wait for Jenkins to download and install the plugins. In the terminal window, you will see log messages as the installation proceeds. Make sure you don't close this terminal window. You can open another terminal window to access the command line.

Step 3. Ignore the creation of a new administrator user.

Once the installation is complete, the **Create First Admin User** window will appear. For now, click **Skip and continue as admin** at the bottom.

Step 4. Ignore the creation of an instance configuration.

In the **Instance Configuration** window, don't change anything and click on **Save and Finish** at the bottom.

Step 5. Start using Jenkins.

In the next window, click on **Start using Jenkins**. You should now be on the main dashboard with a **Welcome to Jenkins!** message.

Part 4: Using Jenkins to run a version of your application

The fundamental unit of Jenkins is the job (also known as the project).you can create jobs that perform a variety of tasks, including the following:

o Rëcupërez code from a source code management repository such as GitHub.

o Create an application using a script or a construction tool.

o Packaging an application and running it on a server

Step 1. Create a new task.

a.   Click on the **Create a job** link directly below the **Welcome to Jenkins!** message page. You can also click on **New Item** in the left-hand menu.

b.   In the **Enter an element name** field, enter the name **BuildAppJob**.

c.   In the description, the abbreviation SCM stands for Software Configuration Management, which is a software classification that is responsible for tracking and controlling changes made to software.

d.   Scroll to the bottom and click **OK**.

Step 2. Configure the Jenkins BuildAppJob.

You're now in the configuration window where you can enter details about your job.The tabs at the top are just shortcuts to the sections below.Click on the tabs to explore the options you can configure.For this simple job, all you need to do is add a few configuration details.

e.   Click on the **General** tab, add a description for your job, for example, "**My first Jenkins job.**

f.   Click on the **Source Code Management** tab and click on the **Git** radio button.In the Repository URL field, add your GitHub repository link for the sample application, taking care to enter your case-sensitive username.Make sure you add the .git extension to the end of your URL. For example :

https://github.com/github-nom_utilisateur/sample-app.git

g.   For **Credentials** click on the **Add** button and choose **Jenkins**.

h.   In the **Add Credentials** dialog box, enter your GitHub username and password, then click **Add**.

Note: you will receive an error message indicating that the connection has failed. This is because you have not yet selected the login details.

i.   In the **Credentials** drop-down list, where it currently says **None**, choose the credentials you have just configured.

j.   After adding the correct URL and credentials, Jenkins tests access to the repository.You should not get an error message.If you do, check your URL and credentials.You will need to **Add** them again.

because there's no way at this stage of deleting the ones you've already got.

k.   At the top of the **BuildAppJob** configuration window, click on the **Build** tab.

l.   For the **Add build step** drop-down list, choose **Execute shell**.

m.   In the **Command** field, enter the command you are using to exëcute the build script for sample-app.sh.

bash./sample-app.sh

n. Click on the **Save** button and you will be returned to the Jenkins dashboard with the **BuildAppJob** selected.

Step 3. Tell Jenkins to build the application.

On the left-hand side, click **Build Now** to start the job.Jenkins will download your Git repository and execute the build command **bash ./sample-app.sh**.Your build should succeed because you haven't changed anything in the code since part 3 when you modified the code.

Step 4. Access the construction details.

On the left, in the **Build History** section, click on your build number, which should be #1 unless you have created the application several times.

Step 5. Display the console output.

On the left, click **Console Output**.you should see a result similar to the following.note the success messages at the bottom and the output of the **docker ps - a** command.two docker containers are running: one for your sampling application running on local port 5050 and one for Jenkins on local port 8080.

Started by user admin
Running as SYSTEM
Building in workspace /var/jenkins_home/workspace/BuildAppJob
using credential 0cf684ea-48a1-4e8b-ba24-b2fa1c5aa3df
Cloning the remote Git repository
Cloning repository https://github.com/github-user/sample-app
>   git init /var/jenkins_home/workspace/BuildAppJob # timeout=10
Fetching upstream changes from https://github.com/github-user/sample-app
>   git -version # timeout=10
using GIT_ASKPASS to set credentials
>   git fetch -tags -progress - https://github.com/github-user/sample-app +refs/heads/*:refs/remotes/origin/* # timeout=10
>   git config remote.origin.url https://github.com/github-user/sample-app # timeout=10
>   git config -add remote.origin.fetch +refs/heads/*:refs/remotes/origin/* # timeout=10
>   git config remote.origin.url https://github.com/github-user/sample-app # timeout=10
Fetching upstream changes from https://github.com/github-user/sample-app
using GIT_ASKPASS to set credentials
>   git fetch -tags -progress - https://github.com/github-user/sample-app +refs/heads/*:refs/remotes/origin/* # timeout=10
>   git rev-parse refs/remotes/origin/master^A {commit} # timeout=10
>   git rev-parse refs/remotes/origin/origin/master^A {commit} # timeout=10
Checking out Revision 230ca953ce83b5d6bdb8f99f11829e3a963028bf (refs/remotes/origin/master)
>   git config core.sparsecheckout # timeout=10
>   git checkout -f 230ca953ce83b5d6bdb8f99f11829e3a963028bf # timeout=10
Commit message: "Changed port numbers from 8080 to 5050"
>   git rev-list -no-walk 230ca953ce83b5d6bdb8f99f11829e3a963028bf # timeout=10
[BuildAppJob] $ /bin/sh -xe /tmp/jenkins1084219378602319752.sh
+ bash./sample-app.sh
Sending build context to Docker daemon 6.144kB
Step 1/7 : FROM python
-      --> 4f7cd4269fa9
Step 2/7 : RUN pip install flask
-      --> Using cache
-      --> 57a74c0dff93
Step 3/7 : COPY ./static /home/myapp/static/
-      --> Using cache
-      --> aee4eb712490
Step 4/7 : COPY ./templates /home/myapp/templates/
-      --> Using cache

-      --> 594cdc822490
Step 5/7 : COPY sample_app.py /home/myapp/
-      --> Using cache
-      --> a001df90cf0c
Step 6/7 : EXPOSE 5050
-      --> Using cache
-      --> eae896e0a98c
Step 7/7 : CMD python3 /home/myapp/sample_app.py
---> Using cache
---> 272c61fddb45
Successfully built 272c61fddb45
Successfully tagged sampleapp:latest
9c8594e62079c069baf9a88a75c13c8c55a3aeaddde6fd6ef54010953c2d3fbb
CONTAINER ID IMAGE COMMAND CREATED STATUS PORTS NAMES
9c8594e62079 sampleapp "/bin/sh -c 'python ..." Less than a second ago Up Less than a second 0.0.0.0:5050- >5050/tcp samplerunning
e25f233f9363 jenkins/jenkins:lts "/sbin/tini -- /usr/." 29 minutes ago Up 29 minutes 0.0.0.0:8080->8080/tcp, 50000/tcp jenkins_server
Finished: SUCCESS

Step 6. Open another web browser tab and check that the sample application is running.

Enter the local address, **localhost: 5050**.You should see the contents of your index.html affichd in a light steel blue background colour with **You are calling me from 172.17.0.1** affichd as H1.

Part 5. Using Jenkins to test a build

In this part, you'll create a second task that tests the construction to make sure it's working properly.

Note: You must stop and delete the **samplerunning** docker container.

devasc@labvm:~/labs/devnet-src/jenkins/sample-app$ **docker stop samplerunning** samplerunning

devasc@labvm:~/labs/devnet-src/jenkins/sample-app$ **docker stop samplerunning** samplerunning

Step 1. Start a new task to test your sample app.

o.   Return to the Jenkins web browser tab and click on the **Jenkins** link in the top left corner to return to the main dashboard.

p.   Click on the **New Item** link to create a new job.

q.   In the Enter a name field, enter the name **TestAppJob**.

r.   Click on **Freestyle project** as the job type.

s.   Scroll to the bottom and click **OK**.

Step 2. Configure the Jenkins TestAppJob.

t.   Add a description for your work, for example, "My first Jenkins test.

u.   Leave Source Code Management set to **None**.

v.   Click on the **Build Triggers** tab and tick the **Build after other projects are built** box. For **Projects to watch**, enter the name **BuildAppJob**.

Step 3. Write the test script that should run after a stable version of BuildAppJob.

w.   Click on the **Build** tab.

x.   Click on **Add build step** and choose **Execute shell**.

y. Enter the following script.The **if** command must be on a single line, including the ; **then**.This command **grep** the output returned by the cURL command to see if **you call me from 172.17.0.1** is returned.If true, the script exits with a code of 0 which means there are no errors in the **BuildAppJob**.If false, the script exits with a code of 1 which means the

BuildAppJob failed.

```
if curl http://172.17.0.1:5050/ | grep "You are calling me from 172.17.0.1"; then
exit 0
else
exit 1
fi
```

z. Click on **Save**, then on the **Back to Dashboard** link on the left-hand side.

Step 4. Tell Jenkins to run the BuildAppJob again.

aa. Refresh the web page using your browser's refresh button.

bb. For the **BuildAppJob**, click on the build button on the far right (a clock with an arrow).

Step 5. Check that both stains are complete.

If all goes well, you should see the timestamp for the update in the **Last Success** column for **BuildAppJob** and **TestAppJob**. This means that your code for the two tasks has run without error, but you can also check this for yourself.

Note: If the timestamps are not updated, make sure that automatic refresh is enabled by clicking on the link at the top right.

cc. Click on the link for **TestAppJob**.under **Permaliens**, click on the link corresponding to your latest version, then click on **Console Output**.you should see a result similar to the following:

Started by upstream project "BuildAppJob" build number 13

cause originally by:

```
Started by user admin
Running as SYSTEM
Building in workspace /var/jenkins_home/workspace/TestAppJob
[TestAppJob] $ /bin/sh -xe /tmp/jenkins1658055689664198619.sh
+ grep You are calling me from 172.17.0.1
+ curl http://172.17.0.1:5050/
% Total % Received % Xferd Average Speed Time Time Time Current
Dload Upload Total Spent Left Speed
0 0 0 0 0 0 0 0 --:--:-- --:--:-- --:--:-- 0
100 177 100 177 0 0 29772 0 --:--:-- --:--:-- --:--:-- 35400
<h1>You are calling me from 172.17.0.1</h1>
+ exit 0
Finished: SUCCESS
```

dd. You don't need to check that your sample application is running as **TestAppJob** has already done this for you, but you can open a browser tab for **172.17.0. 1:5050** to see that it is running.

Part 6. Creating a pipeline in Jenkins

Although you can currently execute both tasks by simply clicking on the Create Now button for **BuildAppJob**, software development projects are typically much more complex and can benefit greatly from automated builds for the continuous integration of code changes and the continuous creation of development builds ready for deployment.This is the essence of CI/CD.A pipeline can be automated to execute based on a variety of triggers, including periodically, based on a GitHub poll for changes, or from a remotely executed script.However, in this part, you will write a pipeline in Jenkins to execute your two applications every time you click the Pipeline **Build Now** button.

Step 1. Create a Pipeline job.

+ Click on the **Jenkins** link at the top left, then on **New element**.

+- In the **Enter an item name** field, type **SamplePipeline**.

4 Select **Pipeline** as the job type.

+- Scroll to the bottom and click **OK**.

Step 2. Configure the SamplePipeline job.

Л5 At the top, click on the tabs and examine each section of the configuration page.Note that there are a number of different fagons of dëclenching a build.For the **SamplePipeline** job, you'll declench it manually.

+ In the **Pipeline** section, add the following script.

```
node {
stage('Preparation') {
catchError(buildResult: 'SUCCESS') {
sh 'docker stop samplerunning'
sh 'docker rm samplerunning'
}
}
stage ('Build') {
build 'BuildAppJob'
}
stage('Results') {
build 'TestAppJob'
}
J
```

This script performs the following operations:

Distributed or multi-node configurations are intended for larger pipelines than the one you are building in this laboratory and are beyond the scope of this course.

o In the **preparation** phase, **SamplePipeline** will first check that all previous instances of the **BuildAppJob** docker container are stopped and deleted.But if there is no container running yet, you will get an error.Therefore, you use the **catchError** function to catch errors and return a "SUCCESS" value.This will ensure that the pipeline moves on to the next stage.

o In the **Build** stage, **SamplePipeline** will build your **BuildAppJob**.

o In the **Results** stage, **SamplePipeline** will build your **TestAppJob**.

■ Click **Save** and you will be returned to the Jenkins dashboard for the **SamplePipeline** task.

Step 3. Run SamplePipeline.

If you have coded your Pipeline script without error, the **Stage View** should display three green areas with the number of seconds each step took to build. If not, click Configure on the left to return to the **SamplePipeline** configuration and check your Pipeline script.

Step 4. Check the SamplePipeline output.

Click on the most recent build link under **Permaliens**, then click on **Console Output**.You should see a result similar to the following:

```
Started by user admin
Running in Durability level: MAX_SURVIVABILITY
[Pipeline] Start of Pipeline
[Pipeline] node
Running on Jenkins in /var/jenkins_home/workspace/SamplePipeline
[Pipeline] {
[Pipeline] stage
[Pipeline] { (Preparation)
[Pipeline] catchError
[Pipeline] {
[Pipeline] sh
```

```
+ docker stop samplerunning
samplerunning
[Pipeline] sh
+ docker rm samplerunning
samplerunning
[Pipeline] }
[Pipeline] // catchError
[Pipeline] }
[Pipeline] // internship
[Pipeline] stage
[Pipeline] {(Build)
[Pipeline] build (BuildAppJob)
Scheduling project: BuildAppJob
Starting building: BuildAppJob #15
[Pipeline] }
[Pipeline] // internship
[Pipeline] stage
[Pipeline] { (Results)
[Pipeline] build (Building TestAppJob)
Scheduling project: TestAppJob
Starting building: TestAppJob #18
```

Workshop 5. Maven project with Jenkins

Introduction

The aim of a Maven project with Jenkins is to set up continuous integration (CI) to automate the process of building, testing and deploying an application. Maven is used as a project management and build tool, while Jenkins orchestrates the continuous integration stages.

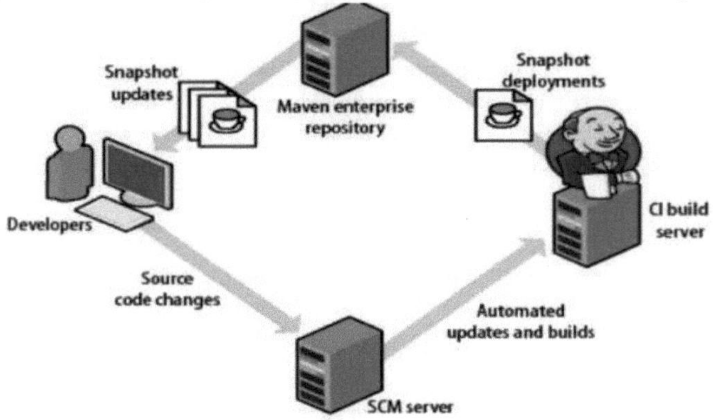

Running a Maven project -

Handling

Step 1: Clone the contents of the project with the git clone command https: //github. com/AbirKaldi/maven-proj ect

Move the content to your github.

Step 2: Install maven on jenkins with the command: docker exec -it jenkins_server apt-get install maven

```
root@Jenkins:/home/jenkins/maven-project# docker exec -it 3edd2140fb0b apt-get install maven
Reading package lists... Done
Building dependency tree... Done
Reading state information... Done
The following additional packages will be installed:
  alsa-topology-conf alsa-ucm-conf ca-certificates-java dbus dbus-bin
  dbus-daemon dbus-session-bus-common dbus-system-bus-common
  default-jre-headless java-common libaopalliance-java libapache-pom-java
  libapparmor1 libasound2 libasound2-data libatinject-jsr330-api-java
  libavahi-client3 libavahi-common-data libavahi-common3 libcdi-api-java
  libcommons-cli-java libcommons-io-java libcommons-lang3-java
  libcommons-parent-java libcups2 libdbus-1-3 liberror-prone-java
  libgeronimo-annotation-1.3-spec-java libgeronimo-interceptor-3.0-spec-java
  libglib2.0-0 libglib2.0-data libgraphite2-3 libguava-java libguice-java
  libharfbuzz0b libicu72 libjansi-java libjpeg62-turbo libjsr305-java
  liblcms2-2 libmaven-parent-java libmaven-resolver-java
  libmaven-shared-utils-java libmaven3-core-java libnspr4 libnss3 libpcsclite1
  libplexus-cipher-java libplexus-classworlds-java
  libplexus-component-annotations-java libplexus-interpolation-java
  libplexus-sec-dispatcher-java libplexus-utils2-java libsisu-inject-java
  libsisu-plexus-java libslf4j-java libwagon-file-java
  libwagon-http-shaded-java libwagon-provider-api-java libxml2
```

Step 3: Launch Jenkins on http://localhost: 8080
Step 4: Create a job with a Maven_Pipeline type name

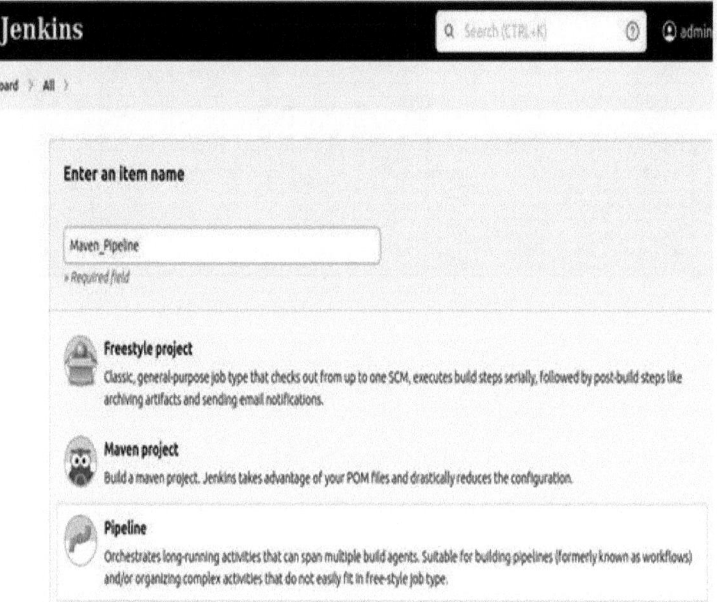

Step 5. Specify 1 github URL

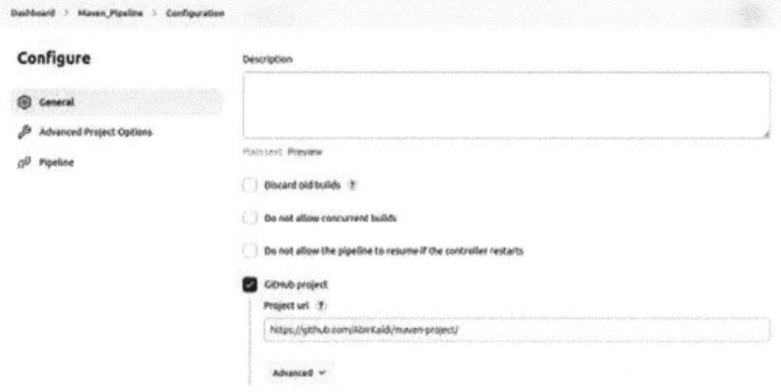

Step 6. Create the pipeline script

```
pipeline {
  agent any

  stages {
    stage('Clean') {
        steps {
          sh 'mvn clean'
        }
    }
    stage('Compile') {
        steps {
          sh 'mvn compile'
        }
    }
    stage('Test') {
        steps {
          sh 'mvn test'
        }
    }
    stage('Package') {
        steps {
          sh 'mvn package'
        }
    }

  }
}
```

Step 7. Launch the pipeline with "Build now

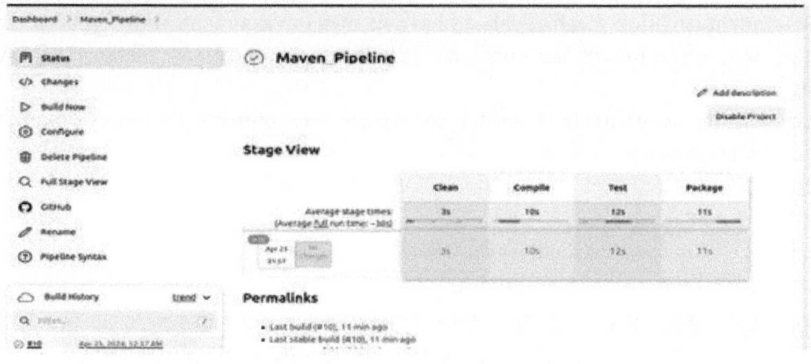

Workshop 6. Jenkins cluster

Introduction

A Jenkins cluster is an architecture in which multiple instances of Jenkins (called newels) are configured to work together, in order to distribute build, test, and dëploiement tasks across multiple machines. This helps to improve performance, manage heavy workloads, and guarantee the high availability of continuous intëgration pipelines.

Here are the main components of a Jenkins cluster:

1.   Jenkins Master (or controller): This is the main instance of Jenkins that дёге task scheduling, monitors build status, distributes jobs to slave newels (agents), and provides the user interface. The master should generally not run builds, but focus on orchestration.

2.   Jenkins Agents (or slaves): These are the machines, virtual or physical, that run builds and tests. The agents are controlled by the master and receive tasks to execute. This makes it possible to parallelise the build process and spread the load over several newels.

3.   Communication between Master and Agents: The master and agents communicate via protocols such as SSH or JNLP (Java Network Launch Protocol). Jenkins sends tasks to the agents and rëcupëre the results once the tasks have been executed.

Advantages of a Jenkins cluster :

4.   Scalability: Allows you to easily add newels to manage more simultaneous builds.

5.   Parallelism: several builds can be run in parallel, reducing the time needed to validate code changes.

6.   Resilience: If one agent goes down, the other nodes continue to work, ensuring greater availability.

7.   Environment isolation: Each agent can have its own environment, allowing projects to be tested and built in different environments (for example, different versions of Java, or operating systëmes).

A Jenkins cluster is particularly useful for large-scale projects requiring complex and intensive CI/CD processes.

Handling

Step 1. Clone the following depot:

git clone https://github.com/AbirKaldi/jenkinsCluster

```
git clone https://github.com/AbirKaldi/jenkinsCluster
```

```
root@jenkins:/home/jenkins/jenkinsCluster
root@jenkins:/home/jenkins# git clone https://github.com/AbirKaldi/jenkinsCluster
loning into 'jenkinsCluster'...
remote: Enumerating objects: 1571, done.
remote: Counting objects: 100% (1571/1571), done.
remote: Compressing objects: 100% (520/520), done.
remote: Total 1571 (delta 969), reused 1571 (delta 969), pack-reused 0
Receiving objects: 100% (1571/1571), 405.55 KiB | 1.80 MiB/s, done.
Resolving deltas: 100% (969/969), done.
root@jenkins:/home/jenkins# ls
jmeter.log
jmeter-server.log
root@jenkins:/home/jenkins# cd jenkinsCluster/
root@jenkins:/home/jenkins/jenkinsCluster# docker compose --profile maven up -d
WARN: The GITPOD_WORKSPACE_URL variable is not set. Defaulting to a blank string.
Creating network "jenkinscluster_default" with the default driver
Creating jenkinscluster sidekick service 1 ... done
Creating jenkinscluster_discovery_and_jcasc_modifier_1 ... done
Creating jenkinscluster jenkins controller 1 ... done
Creating desktop jenkins_agent 1 maven ... done
root@jenkins:/home/jenkins/jenkinsCluster#
```

Step 2. Go to the JenkinsCluster folder and launch the Jenkins cluster with the command :

```
docker-compose --profile maven up -d
```

Step 3. Check that Jenkins containers have been launched with the command :

```
docker ps
```

Step 4. Resume launching the lab3 pipeline on the Jenkins cluster.

Step 5. Launch the pipeline build and check its success.

Step 6. Now stop the desktop-jenkins_agent-1-maven container with the command :

```
docker stop desktop-jenkins_agent-1-maven
```

Step 6. Relaunch the pipeline build and interpret the result.

This book has been designed to give you a complete and practical understanding of DevOps, from its fundamental concepts to its integration into complex environments. Through theoretical explanations and practical workshops, we have explored the tools, methods and technologies that make DevOps an essential approach in the world of modern software engineering. DevOps is not just about specific tools or practices: it's a culture that aims to break down the silos between development and operations teams to encourage collaboration, innovation and the rapid, continuous delivery of quality software. Beyond the technical aspects, this book has also highlighted the importance of human interaction and adapting to feedback to ensure the success of your projects. As you continue your journey into the world of DevOps, remember that learning and improvement are constant. Technologies evolve rapidly, but the fundamental principles of collaboration, automation, and responsiveness to market needs remain essential pillars. We hope that this book has given you the keys not only to mastering the tools, but also to adopting the DevOps mindset in your day-to-day work. The adventure doesn't end here: continue to explore, test and innovate in your DevOps practices to build the future of information systems.

REFERENCES

1. Gene Kim, Jez Humble, Patrick Debois, John Willis - The DevOps Handbook: How to Create World-Class Agility, Reliability, & Security in Technology Organizations (IT Revolution Press, 2016).

2. Emily Freeman- DevOps for Dummies (For Dummies, 2020).

3. Marc Hornbeek - Engineering DevOps: Building World-Class Continuous Delivery Capabilities (Pearson, 2020).

4. Helen Beal - Accelerating DevOps: Transforming IT Operations (Apress, 2021).

5. Jez Humble, David Farley - Continuous Delivery: Reliable Software Releases through Build, Test, and Deployment Automation (Addison- Wesley, 2010).

6. Viktor Farcic - The DevOps 2.3 Toolkit: Kubernetes (Leanpub, 2020).

7. Kief Morris - Infrastructure as Code: Managing Servers in the Cloud (O'Reilly Media, 2020).

8. Stephen Fleming - DevOps: 2 Books in 1 - DevOps for Beginners & DevOps Handbook (Independently published, 2020).

9. Sander Rossel - Continuous Integration, Delivery, and Deployment (Packt Publishing, 2017).

10. Kim W. Ayers - Effective DevOps with AWS: Building a Scalable and Efficient Cloud Infrastructure (Packt Publishing, 2021).

11. Viktor Farcic - The DevOps 2.0 Toolkit: Automating the Continuous Deployment Pipeline with Containerized Microservices (Leanpub, 2016).

12. Ben Straub, Scott Chacon - Pro Git (Apress, 2014).

13. Nathen Harvey, Michael Cote - Chef: The DevOps Workflow (O'Reilly Media, 2017).

14. John Ferguson Smart - BDD in Action: Behavior-Driven Development for the Whole Software Lifecycle (Manning Publications, 2014).

15. Adam Hawkins - DevOps Handbook: Introduction to DevOps and How to Get Started with DevOps (Independently published, 2022).

16. Sam Newman - Building Microservices: Designing Fine-Grained Systems* (O'Reilly Media, 2021).

17. Michael Huttermann - DevOps for Developers: Continuous Integration, Delivery, and Deployment (Apress, 2021).

18. Sean P. Kane, Karl Matthias - Docker: Up & Running: Shipping Reliable Containers in Production (O'Reilly Media, 2020).

yes
I want morebooks!

Buy your books fast and straightforward online - at one of world's fastest growing online book stores! Environmentally sound due to Print-on-Demand technologies.

Buy your books online at
www.morebooks.shop

Kaufen Sie Ihre Bücher schnell und unkompliziert online – auf einer der am schnellsten wachsenden Buchhandelsplattformen weltweit! Dank Print-On-Demand umwelt- und ressourcenschonend produziert.

Bücher schneller online kaufen
www.morebooks.shop

Printed by Books on Demand GmbH, Norderstedt / Germany